CAN DO
Eco-Ventures

Books in the series:

Familiar Things
by Sally Thomas

Eco–Ventures
by Hannah Sugar, Kids' Clubs Network

Serious Fun: Games for 4–9s
by Phill Burton, Dynamix

Whatever the Weather
by Jane Gallagher

Cool Creations
by Mary Allanson, Kids' Clubs Network

Serious Fun: Games for 10–14s
by Phill Burton, Dynamix

Sticks and Stones
by Sharon Crockett

Series Foreword

Children and young people of all ages should be able to initiate and develop their own play. Adult involvement should be based on careful observation, appropriate consultation and response to what the children need in terms of their development at this time and in this place.

Play is freely chosen personally directed behaviour motivated from within. Adults can create the best possible conditions for play: the time, space, materials, safety and support for children to develop the skills and understanding they need to extend the possibilities of their play. The degree to which the children and young people are able to make any activity their own will determine its success as a play opportunity rather than simply 'entertainment', a means of 'keeping them busy' or producing 'something to take home to parents'.

Many of the ideas in these books are not new. Indeed play games and creative activities are passed on across many generations and between different cultures across the world, constantly being adapted and changed to suit a new time, a new group of children, a new environment.

We have acknowledged sources and sought permission wherever it has been possible to do so. We hope, and indeed anticipate, that the ideas in these books will be adapted and developed further by those that use them and would be very interested to hear your comments, thoughts, ideas and suggestions.
www.thomsonlearning.co.uk/childcare

Annie Davy

By Hannah Sugar

Series Editor: Annie Davy

THOMSON

Australia • Canada • Mexico • Singapore • Spain • United Kingdom • United States

THOMSON

Eco-ventures

For more information, contact Thomson, High Holborn House, 50–51 Bedford Row, London, WC1R 4LR or visit us on the World Wide Web at: http://www.thomsonlearning.co.uk

---

British Library Cataloguing-in-Publication Data
A catalogue record for this book is available from the British Library

---

ISBN 1-86152-968-6

First edition 2002

Typeset by Bottle & Co., Banbury, UK

Printed in Croatia by Zrinski

Text design by Bottle & Co.

Contents

Series Introduction

The CAN DO series is an intensely practical resource for children who attend childcare settings, drop in centres or playsettings out of school, and for those of you who work with them in these settings. Anyone working with children, whether as a trainee, an experienced manager or as a volunteer will sometimes get tired, feel jaded or simply seek new inspiration. Whether you are a childminder, a playworker, a family centre worker or a day nursery assistant or manager, you will find a rich source of ideas for children of all ages in the CAN DO series. In these books you will find practical answers to the difficult 'CAN DO' questions which are often asked of adults working with children:

- Child coming in from school, 'What can I do today?'
- Parent visiting a childminder: 'What exactly can the children do here?'
- Playworker or Childcare worker at a team meeting: 'What can we do to extend the range of play provision here?'

The series is structured towards 3 different age ranges—0–3, 4–9 and 10–14, but many of the books will be used successfully by or with older or younger children. The books are written by authors with a wide range of experience in working with children and young people, and who have a thorough understanding of the value of play and the possibilities and constraints of work in childcare and play settings.

Each activity is introduced with a 'why we like it' section, which explains why children and adults who work with children have found this to be something that they enjoyed, or that has enhanced their play provision. Many of the activities also have 'Snapshots' and 'Spotlight' boxes which expand on the possibilities as developed by children, or an approach you can take in working with children. These sections are intended to help you reflect on your work and the quality of what is provided.

The ideas in this series are intended to be playful, inclusive and affordable. They are not based on any prescribed curriculum, but they could be used to enrich and develop almost any setting in which children play and learn. They do not rely on expensive toys and equipment; they are environmentally friendly and are peppered with practical tips and health and safety checkpoints.

Language used in the book

YOU (the reader): The books are addressed to children and the adults who work with them together. Older children will be able to use the books themselves or with a little co-operation from adults. There are some activities where adult supervision or assistance will be required (in developing and supervising safe working with tools for example) and this is highlighted where relevant.

SETTING: We have used the term 'setting' rather than club, scheme, centre, etc. as the generic term to describe the range of contexts for childcare and playwork including childminders' homes. The 'Snapshot' draw on a range of different settings to illustrate the development of some of the activities in practice.

PLAYLEADER: This term is predominantly used in the 4–9 and 10–14 series, as this is the most familiar generic term that covers adults working with these age groups in out of school settings.

Eco-ventures

Welcome to Eco-ventures! Roll up your sleeves and get ready to embark on creative and imaginative adventures.

Introduction

Explore the environment through imaginative sculptures, models and a bit of detective work. Interview a tree or realise the capabilities of used materials to create musical instruments. Find out how to make an ice lantern or fragrant coaster out of water using old plastic bottles and lids from jars. Create your own imaginative play spaces in Rocket Journey, On the Bus or travel the world in Passport Check.

Eco-ventures does not hover around leaves and mini-beasts but provides a variety of exciting starting points for children of all ages and abilities to pick up and expand. Navigate the book via the four main sections. Community Detectives, How Does Your Garden Grow, Changing Things and Global Eco-ventures.

Choose to suit your mood and the time you have available - from short, fun activities such as shadow makers or alien encounters to a four week long caterpillar house project. Find ways to recycle and reuse, take turns and join with others in developing new skills and using all your senses. Develop new hobbies and interests such as choosing to take responsibility for the care of living things in the larger projects such as Butterfly Garden, Caterpillar Houses and Compost Maker.

Many of the adventures are illustrated with 'snapshots' of how the ideas have been tried, tested and interpreted by others. Serving both adult and child readers, the Safety Check bulletins remind all when caution is required or when help from an adult is recommended. Each section suggests what you might need in terms of tools and materials. But these are only recommendations for you to adapt and interpret to your own specifications. Most activities can be done with limited resources.

Through your Eco-venture play, you can gain new skills and understanding about the world and each other. You can develop the capacity to follow a plan with an end product in mind, or you might change that plan and take your adventure into new and totally unpredictable directions. Resources such as books and website pages are suggested if you wish to extend your knowledge further. The activities give plenty of practical tips and advice, but they are suggested primarily to stimulate ideas for play opportunities which can be initiated by and developed by children themselves.

Acknowledgements *for Eco-ventures*

I would like to express thanks to everyone who has helped with the preparation of this book:

To those who have contributed their ideas, activity suggestions and tips - Jay Nelson (Rollercoasters Play Centre), Margaret Lowndes (Robins Den before and after school club), Janet Heely (Builth Wells after school club) Treehouse Kids Club, Blue Dragon out of school club, The Vine Play Centre, Ros Patching (RSPB), Lucy Williams, (artist). To Ed and my mum for their support.

The Rocket Journey, On the Bus and Gravity Art were inspired by Rollercoasters Play Centre. Compost Maker, Interview a Tree and Alien Encounters were inspired by the RSPB Elemental Suitcase. Sparkle Paper was inspired by Lucy Williams.

Butterfly Garden was inspired by the Blue Dragon out of school club. Community Collage was inspired by Kids' Clubs Week 2001 Action Pack, Kids' Clubs Network. Music from Junk was inspired by School's Out! Get Active.

Kids' Clubs Network is the national membership organisation for school age childcare. The organisation undertakes a wide range of activities to develop and support all aspects of childcare and out of school activities for children, parents and communities. For more information *www.kidsclubs.org.uk* or call the information line on 020 7512 2100.

Photography on page 41 reproduced with kind permission of The Vine Play Centre and Kids' Clubs Network.

Photography on page 53 reproduced with kind permission of Margaret Lowndes.

Community Collage

Why we like it

Create a picture of your community in a giant collage. This activity helps you get to know your environment and the community you live in—the good and the bad. The collage is great fun and encourages imagination and creativity as you explore ways to illustrate your community. It is interesting to decide what features to include.

What you might need

Large sheet of paper or card

Pencils

Glue and sticky tape

Paints and wax crayons

Materials to use to recreate your local environment such as leaves, twigs, pebbles and bus tickets!

How many can do it

2 or more depending on the size of your collage.

Where can you do it

Find a large table or space on the floor. All children will need to reach the paper to add to the collage.

How you can do it

1. Draw a simple map of your community on a large sheet of paper. Include roads, streams and buildings. What buildings do you think should be included? Your house, kids' club or playcentre may come top of the list! Include things that are important to each participant such as the swings, trees, play areas or even bus stops.

2. Share ideas on how you will represent these features—what materials will you use to illustrate the school playground or the swimming pool? You might collect materials from your environment such as twigs, feathers or train tickets. Use wax crayons and paper to take rubbings from trees, bark or street signs. Collect till receipts and leaflets from your local shops, bus tickets and leaflets from your school. Look around you and find objects that reflect what makes up your local area. If there is litter, collect some—it can tell you a lot about your community.

3. You can now glue or tape your findings to the map. Use your imagination and creativity to illustrate the local area. If you are a big group, perhaps work in smaller groups to concentrate on certain parts of the map making sure everyone's contributions can be included.

4. Stand back and enjoy the creation of your community collage.

Safety Check

When collecting litter, ensure the children are wearing protective gloves. Adult supervision is needed to explain what can and cannot be safely used—pay close attention to what the children are touching.

Useful Tips

Allow plenty of time for planning what should be included—this might be walking around your local community, looking at pictures, taking photos or just comparing notes about favourite places and things to do.

Snapshot

Treehouse after school club in Newcastle enjoy making collages. When their playleader suggested making a collage to illustrate the importance of their local community in relation to their out of school club, they approached it with enthusiasm. The centre of the display was the club's logo, designed by the children. Things that were of importance within the local area were then placed around their logo. They picked their favourite places—where they like to go and what they like to see. The beach is important to the club so they collected shells and sand and used blue paper and material to represent the sea.

What next?

Encourage discussions about the local environment perhaps look at likes and dislikes. Add comments to the collage such as what features are liked and how other features of the environment could be improved. What would you like to change?

Display the collage at your setting. If you do not have a permanent premises approach the library or town hall and ask if they could display it.

Take a photograph of the collage and when you repeat this activity in the future look at the similarities and differences in the features and how the children have chosen to illustrate them.

Tree Tales

Why we like it

This is an activity needing few props. It encourages imagination and communication and can be done in a spare 10 minutes or you can extend it and elaborate into a bigger project. It is a lively introduction to recognising trees and making them interesting as well as thinking about what life must have been like in the past. This activity introduces interviewing and journalism.

What you might need

Props for dressing up

A tree to focus on

Notepad and pencil or a tape recorder with a microphone for recording interviews.

How many can do it

A minimum of 2 participants. 2–6 for each interview or have several pairs or small groups taking part.

Where you can do it

Best done out of doors where there are some real trees (although possible to set up indoors).

How you can do it

1. In this activity you need to identify a tree and tell its story to a journalist (your partner). Trees are the largest and longest living things on land. Imagine what a tree has seen during its lifetime and what might it say of it could speak?

2. Think about trees in your community especially the oldest and biggest ones you have noticed. You could investigate how long the tree has been alive.

3. Once you have chosen a tree start imagining what that tree will have seen. How old do you think the tree is?

4. After talking together researching and imagining the tree and how your community has changed, get together in pairs or very small groups. One of you will be the journalist. Perhaps dress up to help your character. The other partner is the tree. Make costumes, draw leaf shapes on green paper and attach the leaves to your jumper with sticky tape. This is an opportunity for face painting if you have the time.

5. Get reporting. If there are several pairs taking part, group all the journalists together to think about possible questions and likewise the trees to think about what they have seen.

6. The journalists must now visit their tree and conduct an interview. Only the journalist has to write in this activity so the pairs can be of mixed age and ability. Or you can use a tape recorder if available. You might ask the tree how old it is and what things it has seen during its life. What changes has the tree seen? What about the cars passing beneath it—can it remember horses and carts? What does the tree like? What does the tree dislike?

7. Ask the journalists to return to the news desk and each journalist to report back highlights of their story to the Editor and the rest of the group.

Useful Tip

Practice interviewing in lots of ways. Watch TV clips, read magazine interviews to think of good questions.
Look at trees and photographs of your local area in books to find out what your tree might have seen.

Spotlight—On Trees

Investigate how long the tree has been alive. The Yew tree is a medium sized evergreen with red berries and can live as long as 2000 years! The most common tree in Great Britain is the Oak tree and this can have a lifespan of 1000 years. You may recognise the Silver Birch, this tree has a shorter life expectancy of 60 years. Did you know, 284 species of insects can live on a single oak tree!

Snapshot

Sally age 7 Journalist
Cara age 5 tree

Sally: How long have you lived in Framlingham?
Cara: for 100 years.
Sally: Do you like living here?
Cara: I have lots of friends who say hello to me.
Sally: Who are your friends?
Cara: The ducks from the pond, the postman on his bike, the children going to school and the man who sweeps the pavement.
Sally: What was it like 50 years ago?
Cara: There were no cars and people wore hats everyday!
Sally: Does anything upset you?
Cara: I don't like the rubbish left at my feet, it gets smelly but the sweeper man tidies up which is good.
Sally: I'm Sally for the six o'clock news talking to the old oak tree.

What next?

This activity may spur new interest in trees. You could take rubbings of bark and leaves. Find out what animals live around the tree?

Your group might want to help preserve local trees or plant a tree.

Contact the planning department at your local council for ideas and help.

Depending on the extent you research the history of your community you might develop other interests to follow up with crafts, drama and games.

Or you might develop further skills in interviewing other topics.

On the Bus

What you might need

2 large sheets of Poly-board, 3 m by 1.5 m

4 carpet rolls, each 60 cm long—ask at a carpet shop

Cardboard

Pieces of Willow

Scissors

Poster paints

Plasticine

Wool

PVA glue

Masking tape

Tape recorder.

Why we like it

You can celebrate a journey with On the Bus. You can use lots of recycled materials and be creative with the construction and decoration of your vehicle sculpture. It also involves thinking of songs and games to play when on the bus.

How many can do it

3–7.

How you can do it

1. Cut the two sheets of Poly-board to the basic shape of the bus. Leave extra board around the edges and on the top, this will be used later.

2. The carpet rolls will hold the two sides of the bus together at the bottom. Hold the sides of the bus upright and in line with about 30 cm between them. Measure the diameter of the carpet rolls and mark onto the Poly-board where the rolls should slot. Carefully cut out the holes.

3. Hold the sides of the bus upright—at least two people will need to do this. Push the carpet rolls through the holes with at least 10 cm poking out either side of the bus. To make the frame stronger, wrap each carpet roll in cardboard to act as a buffer and prevent the roll from bending. Where the rolls stick out either side, make holes and push willow through to strengthen and steady the ends. The overlap will hold the bus like feet, see Fig 3

4. The top, front and back of the bus are now open. Bend the Poly-board to follow the shape of the bus. Cut tabs and slots so the pieces of board slot together.

5. Get decorating! Look at the features of your bus and recreate them on your sculpture. With felt pens draw an outline of the lights, windows, number plate, fuel cap etc.. Paint on the graphics of your bus and fill in all the details. Perhaps use materials such as tissue paper, foil or cloth as well as paints. The main feature will be the faces of the passengers on the bus. You can draw straight onto the bus or make faces to stick on.

6. Go on a real bus ride and take your tape recorder. Record the sounds of the bus and the voices of the passengers.

7. Link your tape recorder to the bus sculpture, perhaps put the tape recorder inside the bus. Cut a door in the back of the bus and pierce some small holes in the side of the bus to help amplify the sound.

Safety Check

If your tape recorder is plugged into the mains make sure you tape down the lead so it cannot trip a passer-by.

Adult supervision and assistance will be needed when cutting the Poly-board and carpet rolls.

Snapshot

To celebrate their new minibus, Fun Club in Barnsley made a sculpture. The children wanted to do something more creative than draw pictures of the bus so they worked out how to make an indoor minibus. The children wanted to be able to play in the bus so a wider version of the bus construction was made with a window cut out at the front and two chairs placed inside so the minibus could have drivers. Driving the bus is now a popular imaginative activity with many of the children. You might find Kevin and Malin driving together. While Kevin steers, Malin is often pressing buttons and turning switches as if in an aeroplane cockpit. Sharma has made a zebra crossing and pretends to be a lollipop lady in front of the minibus. Some other children have made a scrapbook full of games, songs and activities to do when on a minibus journey. This book now travels everywhere with the club. Using a tape recorder, Kanice and Fiona interviewed the other children before they got on the minibus. They recorded sounds of the engine and the chatter of the children on a journey. They narrated the safety checks and recorded the sound of seatbelts clicking into place. With the help of an older brother, Kanice and Fiona edited the tape providing a great 'soundtrack' documentary to the journey.

Useful Tips

When drawing your faces put masking tape around the window frame. This helps keep the passengers inside the bus!

You can get Poly-board from arts and crafts suppliers or ask at your local scrapstore. Alternatively you can make a smaller sculpture using large pieces of cardboard (flattened boxes) and cardboard rolls. You may need to reinforce the sculpture using chicken wire.

What next?

When your sculpture is complete exhibit the bus in your play setting. Perhaps have a travel theme for your games and activities.

If you are unable to keep the bus in your play setting ask your local library, town hall or school to exhibit it.

Make a scrapbook of ideas of things would like to do on a bus journey.

Paint pictures and make collages of the bus sculpture.

Alien Encounters

Why we like it

Can you promote your area and sell it to an alien to make them want to stay. It is easy to take for granted the things around you but this game helps view the world from a new perspective.
Your imagination can go wild! It promotes communication and using language effectively.

What you might need

Pens and crayons
Dressing up clothes and materials (optional)
Watch or clock.

How many can do it

2–20.

Where we can do it

Indoors or outdoors.

How you can do it

1. Aliens from outer space have crash landed outside your play setting. The aliens have taken on human form and need to find out how to survive. Divide yourselves into aliens and earthlings.

2. The aliens have only five minutes to decide whether to stay on earth or return to their home planet, the space craft will dissipate in 300 seconds! Aliens need to quickly think what questions they are going to ask to help them decide.

3. Each alien picks an earthling to ask his or her questions.

4. Stop the interviews after five minutes. Group together and find out if the aliens have decided to stay or whizz off back into space. How have the aliens been persuaded or not?

Questions to ask the earthlings:

What are you made from?
What do you eat?
Where do you get your food from?
Are there any other creatures living on the Earth?
What do you live in?
Do you build your own homes?
Who do you choose to live with?
How do you travel?
What makes you happy?

What next?

Create costumes and use face paints to help you get into character.

Create a home planet for the aliens and create a language and distinguishing features of the alien kind.

Use the information created to spur imagination for paintings, pictures and stories.

Adapt one of your favourite active games to an alien theme.

Try playing Escape From the Planet Of 'What'

This game needs some advance preparation, so allow lots of time. A small group could plan and prepare the clues and tasks for another group who want to be aliens (perhaps the following day).

It can be played in teams or as individuals or in pairs. At least one participant must be the clue master to answer the aliens' questions and help them find their spaceship.

Each participant is an alien and needs to find his or her spaceship. A clue will lead the aliens to their spaceship. A message at the spaceship informs the aliens that their spaceship has malfunctioned and they have crashed on the Planet of 'What '. They have 10 minutes to follow the clues that will lead them to a new spaceship. Clues can be drawings, written clues or verbal clues. These will have been prepared before the game.

On the Planet of 'What' the aliens are only able speak with sentences beginning with 'who', 'what' or 'where.' The clue master can provide answers to any who, what or where questions. Clues lead the aliens from station to station where they have to perform a task (such as making up a national anthem for the planet, or crawling through a laser field). The final task could be to build a spaceship out of any equipment available.

Bird Watching

Why we like it

The opportunity to observe birds closely can develop curiosity and motivation to find out more about the living world around you. Birds are an accessible resource, almost everywhere and can stimulate a range of play opportunities—from imaginative games to creative activities and artwork.

What you might need

Cardboard tubes

Sticky tape

Drawing and painting paper

Large clear pictures of birds for reference

Scissors

Binoculars (optional).

To make a bird watching 'hide' indoors

A window

Coloured paper to cover the window.

To make a bird watching 'hide' outdoors

A climbing frame

Dull coloured material to cover the frame

Mat or rug to sit on.

How many can do it

1–6

Smaller groups are better for this activity.

Where to do it

Find a suitable site to bird watch, could be indoors looking through a window or outdoors in the play area under a climbing frame.

How you can do it

1. Make a bird 'hide' to view birds close up. Where have you seen birds and what kind of places do birds like? Find a place to watch, looking out for evidence that birds might come and visit—are there bushes with berries which attract blackbirds, thrushes and sparrows or trees and hedges? Think about the requirements for your bird hide including the comfort needs of the 'watchers'.

2. To make a bird hide from a window you need to screen yourselves from the birds. Cover the window with dark coloured paper by using see-through sticky tape to attach the paper to the glass. Use masking tape when attaching to paint work. You don't need to cover the whole window, cover it to the height of the watchers.

3. How are you going to watch the birds? Sat at a table or standing at the window? Mark on the paper and carefully cut out viewing slots at various heights. Cut out the slots before securing the paper screen to the window.

4. Stick up information to your screen about birds and decorate your bird watching hide.

Safety Check

Wear rubber gloves when washing out the bird bath.

Don't look directly at the sun and be especially careful not to look at the sun through the binoculars.

Wash your hands after touching feathers.

5. Sit or stand quietly at your hide and watch what birds come to visit your grounds. What are the birds doing? What is their favourite food? Look at the colourings, sizes and shapes of the birds.

6. Keep a chart of the birds you see each session, paint pictures of the birds you see and make models.

7. Develop your watching area to attract more birds. For example, leave areas of uncut grass to attract seed eating birds such as bullfinches and birds interested in insects like swallows. Short grass is good for blackbirds and thrushes to find worms.

8. Make a bird bath out of a dustbin lid or shallow bowl for the birds to drink from and bathe, sink the lid into the ground or place on bricks. Keep the bird bath clean and change the water regularly. When it is cold, put a small ball in the water to prevent the whole bath from freezing over. This is particularly important during winter months when usual water sources are frozen or dry in the summer.

Spotlight—Focus on Birds

Recent surveys have indicated that the following birds have been regular visitors to many sites across the UK: chaffinch, black-headed gull, collard dove, jackdaw, magpie, sparrow, starling, siskin, robin, rook, great tit, blue tit, greenfinch, song thrush, woodpigeon, wren and blackbird. Most of these birds feed on the ground so you should be able to get a good look at them.

The male blackbird is black with a bright yellow bill. Blackbirds often hop along the ground and eat apples, berries and worms. The house sparrow, great tit and starling will feed from nut feeders. The starling is a noisy bird and will look black in the distance. Up close the starling is green and purple with white spots. Magpies are large black and white birds with a long tail, you may see them in pairs or groups.

Useful Tips

The morning is the best time to watch for birds as they come out to feed after the cold night.

Use pictures to help you recognise and identify the visiting birds. Take a look at *www.rspb.org.uk* for bird identification material, games and information or look at *Birds,* Usborne Spotter's Guides; *Birds*, Ladybird Discovery.

Snapshot

The breakfast club starts at 7.30 at Happy Times Club in Suffolk. In the spring the children took on the challenge of making a bird watch in the grounds of the primary school. The children decided their bird watch should be behind the library wall where there is a hedge, an old tree and a medium sized patch of grass. They carried round the climbing frame the club use indoors and covered it with the parachute. Rather than cutting holes in the parachute they attached a large piece of cardboard to the front of the frame with string. Their playworker cut viewing slots and holes in the cardboard. Inside the bird watch they put the reading mat on the ground and a chair for Harry. They have started a chart for anyone who watches the birds in their hide. The children borrow books from the library about birds and paint pictures and make models of the birds they most often see. The younger members enjoy picking up feathers and using them in collages and other craft activities. The hide has to be brought in before school everyday but is kept in the club room. On rainy mornings and afternoons the children meet in the hide, indoors, to catch up on their chart and generally chat with one another. All the children have picked up that they need to be reasonably quiet when in the hide and have a lot of respect for the hide which they designed and look after. The school are happy to let the bird watching area grow wild to encourage more birds to visit.

What next?

Add features to your bird watch and make equipment such as binoculars out of cardboard tubes. As birds are regularly seen find out what they eat and where they nest and shelter. If possible, make changes to the environment to help keep the birds returning. For example, if the birds enjoy eating the berries on a hedge find out if the hedge can be pruned less often. Put up some bird boxes and make a bird table. If you provide food for the birds you will need to continue to do so as the birds may rely on you as a source of food.

Use pictures of birds, or a bird 'lotto' game to play matching games to identify the different types of birds and their names. Have you seen any of these birds from your hide?

Take part in the RSPB's Big Garden Birdwatch, an annual survey of garden birds each January. For more details call RSPB Education on 01767 680551.

Shining Stars

Why we like it

Inventing robots and travelling in space are hot topics for many youngsters. Discovering the night sky can open up whole new worlds of exploration, curiosity and interest. It is a great starting point for all kinds of imaginative play. You can adapt these suggestions here to shorter or longer activities to suit the ages, abilities and interests of those taking part.

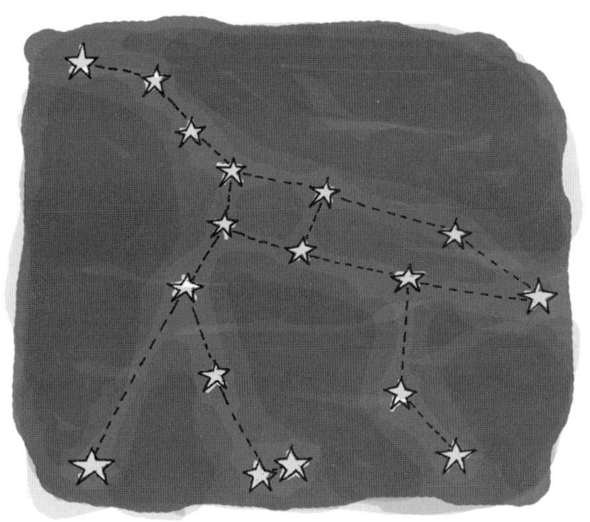

Fig.1

What you might need

Some aluminium foil

Cardboard tube, one each (kitchen roll tube is best)

Torch, one between two or three

Red cellophane approximately 20 cm by 20 cm depending on the size of your torch

Pebbles

Deep sided tray

Plaster of Paris

Jug of water

Newspaper

Notepad

Pens, pencils and paints for decoration.

How many can do it

1–12.

Where you can do it

Star gazing needs a clear night out of doors, preferably in the winter months when it gets darker earlier. Make star viewers and lunar landscapes indoors.

How you can do it

Stargaze

1. On a winter evening, wrap up warm and go outside to watch the stars. Cover your torches with red cellophane to act as a filter and diffuse the white light. This will help your eyes get used to seeing in the dark. Looking up into the sky what can you see? Can you pick out patterns of stars? Are there bright stars and twinkling stars? Can you see the moon, what shape is it? Do you know what any of the stars are called or the shapes of any of the constellations?

2. When you get indoors see if you can remember any of the constellations. Use a reference book or web site to find out more.

3. Cut a piece of tin foil 20 cm by 20 cm to cover one end of the cardboard tube. Attach the foil by moulding it around the tube, making sure the foil over the hole is flat and taught. Secure the foil with sticky tape. Alternatively tie with string or an elastic band.

4. Using a drawing pin carefully prick holes in the foil to match the pattern of stars from a constellation (see Fig.1)

5. Hold the star viewer to the light and observe your star constellation.

How you can do it

Lunar landscape

1. When you looked at the moon, did you notice the craters? These craters were created by meteorites when the moon was first formed. To create your own lunar landscape, first make some meteorites. Wrap one or two small pebbles in foil and make them as round as possible.

2. Line a deep-sided tray or dish tray with foil and place it on some sheets of newspaper on the floor. Empty plaster of Paris into the tray and spread evenly.

3. Pour water from a jug carefully into the powder stirring all the time. If the plaster is too thin add some more powder.

4. Let the plaster thicken but not set and get ready to bombard your lunar surface. Stand around your tray and hold the meteorites at chest height. Carefully drop them into the plaster.

5. Remove the meteorites and allow the plaster to set.

Useful Tips

If you can't get out to see the night sky, borrow some books from the library to find out about star constellations.

When outside wrap your torches in red cellophane to help you see in the dark.

Stir the plaster until you are ready to drop the meteorites, to prevent the plaster from setting. This is best done on the floor with newspaper covering the floor and children wearing aprons. It is good to make the plaster in pairs so they can swap regularly when stirring.

Snapshot

Masumo, Casper and Jenny often bring rockets and robots into their play so during the winter months when it was dark and dingy Alison, their childminder, decided to hold a space party. In the week or two leading up to the party the children were involved in the planning, and started using space as a theme in their games and crafts. They looked through picture books and searched the Internet for space information. Paintings included rockets, the moon and green aliens.

On the day of the party, when the children walked through the door after school they saw the kitchen table full of exciting materials. Each child had a torch and covered it with squares of red tissue paper. Most of the party was lit by the filtered re-chargeable torches and a lamp, decorated as an alien, providing extra light. The children had picked up the idea of star constellations earlier in the week and thoroughly enjoyed looking for them in the sky. They each noted a star pattern they liked the best and used it to make their star viewer which they could take home. They made a name for their star constellation and decorated the viewer with silver star stickers and drawings of the moon, sun and earth.

After the children embarked on creating they own lunar landscapes. Masumo and Casper revelled in making meteorites while Jenny mixed the plaster of Paris in the foil-lined tray. The three of them stood around the tray and one by one dropped the meteorites into the plaster.

What next?

Make some aliens and a spacecraft to land on your lunar landscape out of paper plates, yoghurt pots, cardboard rolls and pipe cleaners.

Keep a diary of the moon and watch how it changes shape during a month.

Find information about the planets in our universe and make models out of papier mache.

Dress up as Astronauts and aliens.

Play Alien Encounters on page 10.

Take a look at resource books to boost your space know how:

Sun, Stars & Planets by Tom Stacy, 1990, Kingfisher, London

Skywatch by Rhoda Nottridge, *et al,* 1991, Harper Collins, London

The Young Astrologer by Harry Ford, 1998, Dorling Kindersley, London

Space and Spaceflight by Harry Ford, 1994, Puffin, London

Miniature Growing Garden

Why we like it

This activity is great for individuals and larger groups. It can be achieved in a day, a couple of play sessions or can be spread over days and weeks if you plant seeds. It is great fun designing the garden and watching it grow. This activity raises awareness of the environment, helps develop understanding of how plants grow and encourages imagination and creativity.

What you might need

Old washing up bowl or seed tray
Clean plastic bottle or carton
Lolly sticks
Compost
Pebbles
Seeds
Twigs
Moss
Cardboard
Paint
Paper
Pencils
Scissors
Modelling clay.

How many can do it

1–6
Each participant can make their own garden or work in pairs.

Where you can do it

Either indoors or outdoors being aware that you will have lots of material.

Safety Check

Make sure you wash your hands after handling soil or plants.
Adult help may be needed when cutting plastic bottles.

How you can do it

1. The first stage in the miniature growing garden activity is to become garden designers. To design a garden you should begin with a large sheet of paper or card on which you will draw your design. The size of the garden will be determined by the size of tray you will use in the next step. Each designer will have his or her own ideas and features. You will need to think about the type of garden: for example will you have a wooden planked area such as decking or do you want pebbles or gravel? Will you have a water feature? Will you have plants, fences or hedges? Will you have a summerhouse, a swing or a vegetable patch? Draw in any water features, paths, decking or plant areas. Take your inspiration from TV makeovers, gardening magazines, local gardens.

2. Once your designs are ready you can now become landscape gardeners and create your own gardens. The washing-up bowl or seed tray will act as the base of the garden. Part-fill the tray with potting compost. Using your designs mark out and fill any path areas with pebbles.

3. Plant some seeds into the compost and watch your garden grow. Mustard and cress grow quickly and will soon be creating lots of greenery. If it is spring and you have more time, plant some runner beans or other fast growing seeds. Remember to plant the seeds where you want them to grow following your garden design.

4. Some gardens may include a water feature. To create a pond cut off the bottom of a clean plastic bottle and submerge it into the soil. To create decking, glue together lolly sticks and lay on top of the soil. Other garden designs may include a vegetable patch. Make some beanpoles from twigs tied with thread and press firmly into the soil. Use moss to create a hedge or twigs or lolly sticks to construct a fence. Add larger stones for a dramatic effect especially good for gardeners creating a desert garden.

5. Once the layout of the garden is ready you can then move on to garden furniture. Use lolly sticks, twigs and card to create garden seats, a garden shed or summerhouse. You may want to consider providing an area of shade from the sun.

6. Painting and decorating is the next step. Paint fences and sheds, fill the pond with water. Make flower pots out of modelling clay. Using your imagination, collect miniature objects to add to the garden. Remember to lightly water the compost to keep your plants alive.

What next?

When the landscape gardeners are ready and happy with their creations why not hold a garden show? Display your gardens to family, friends or your community

You could continue the garden theme and try growing your own food or creating a butterfly garden (see page 27).

Useful Tips

Don't forget to water the garden. Perhaps suggest a team of 'gardeners' take responsibility for this task.

Talk about maintaining your garden and caring for the plants.

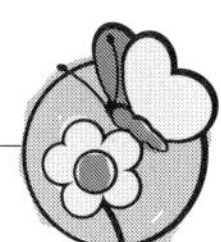

Create your own Compost

Why we like it

Making your own plant food is a great activity to introduce soil, plants and how plant matter recycles itself in compost. The activity encourages you to care for plants and take an interest in gardening. It is a good activity to link with growing plants or recycling activities. The compost maker is simple to make and can last a number of months.

What you might need

Two big plastic drink bottles (lids removed)

A craft knife

Glue or strong tape

A hot skewer

A very small amount of garden compost

Finely chopped scraps of raw fruit and vegetables—carrot tops, potato peels, apples cores.

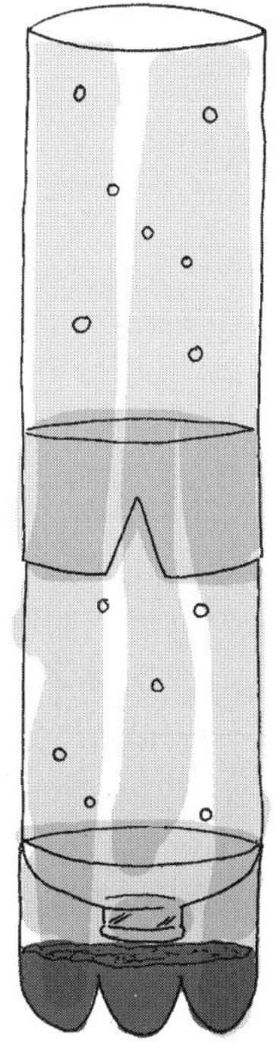

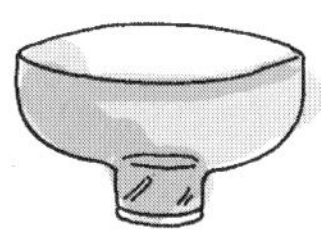

Safety Check

This activity requires a lot of cutting plastic bottles which will need adult supervision and assistance.

Adults needed to use the hot skewer

Wash your hands after touching compost

How many can do it

1–3 per compost maker.

Where you can do it

This is an indoor way of making compost to allow you to observe what happens in a compost heap.

How you can do it

1. Cut the bottom off one of the bottles 12 cm from the base. Cut the top and bottom off the other bottle (you will not need the bottom of this bottle).

2. Cut a small triangle out of the middle part of the second bottle. Stick the middle part of this bottle onto the long, top part of the first bottle and fix them together with glue or tape. This is the tower.

3. Add a small amount of garden compost into the 12 cm high bottle bottom.

4. Attach the tower on top of this with the bottle top facing downwards and carefully drop in fruit and vegetable scraps.

5. Place the spare bottle top upside down on top of the tower to act as a lid.

6. Get an adult to pierce lots of holes in the tower using the heated end of a skewer. These holes will allow air to get in.

7. Leave the tower on a window sill or in a garden shed for about three weeks.

8. After three weeks, enough liquid compost should have drained into the bottom of your compost maker to provide some great house plant food. Dilute it with water before you put it on plants.

Spotlight—Soil as Food

When we grow flowers and vegetables, nutrients are taken out of the soil to feed the plants . When we take plants out of the soil, such as a crop of potatoes, we leave very little vegetation to rot down and make humus which helps keep the soil fertile. To put humus back into the soil we need to make compost.

Millions of tiny animals live in the soil and are also very important as they keep soil full of nutrients. There are about three million earthworms in every acre of grassland and they can live for 10 years!

Snapshot

Alicia and Chen found great delight in becoming the garden compost monitors! Following another project at the after school club where the children planted hanging baskets and tubs for the school courtyard, they were eager to continue with their greenfingers tasks. The compost maker was a great construction activity in which the three youngsters showed incredible teamwork, patience and commitment. They prepared raw carrots, lettuce leaves, used apple and satsuma peel left over from snack times. The compost has been feeding the garden area and Alicia and Chen's interest has attracted other children to take part in weeding, watering and generally maintaining the courtyard. A local gardening shop has donated some gardening tools and seedlings.

Sprouting Seeds

Why we like it

This is an age-old activity but being able to watch the germination of a seed and a plant growing is always magical. Sprouting seeds is easy to do, requires several sessions but very few props.

What you might need

Empty and clean clear glass or plastic jars

Cotton wool

Shoe boxes with lids

Plastic tray or dish to fit inside shoe box

Paper towel

Cress seeds

Bean or another seed no smaller than a pea in size

Dark coloured paper or card

Pens and pencils.

How many can do it

1–15.

Where can we do it

Indoors.

Useful Tips

Keep the jar and box in a warm light place.

Put your name on your box and jar.

Remember to water both the seed and the cress seeds regularly but do not drown them.

How you can do it

1. Look at your seed, it has a hard covering. Inside your seed's protective covering is the beginning of a whole new plant. All your seed needs now is the correct conditions to grow such as moisture and oxygen.

2. Dampen pieces of cotton wool and put inside your clean jar. Rest your seed on top of the cotton wool. Make sure you can see the seed. Write your name on a small piece of paper and tape it to your jar. Place your jar in a warm and light place and monitor the seed's growth every time you are at your play setting. Perhaps give your seed a name.

3. While your seed is germinating in the jar, plant some cress. Layer your tray with damp paper towels and sprinkle some cress seeds. Put your seeds in the shoebox. The shoebox will act as a greenhouse to help your cress seeds germinate and grow. Cut a window in the lower half of one end and close the lid. You might want to write or draw a brief diary about how it grows.

4. Keep your shoebox greenhouse in a warm, light place and keep the seeds moist with water. Keep monitoring your cress crop and watch how it grows and in what direction.

5. In the jar the seed will be absorbing the water from the cotton wool, the cells of the embryo will start to divide and expand inside the protective covering. The cover will split as the new plant grows. The first thing to appear will be a little white root. What direction does it grow? Soon after another shoot will appear but this shoot will grow upwards. This shoot will grow into the stem of your new plant.

6. When your plant grows bigger, plant it in some soil in a pot.

Spotlight—Seed Germination

The first thing to appear from your seed is a small white root, the radical. The root always grows first and downwards in search of water and nutrients. Did your root grow downwards? The second shoot to appear from your seed will always grow upwards in search for sunlight and oxygen. This shoot will grow into the stem of the new plant.

What next?

Before sowing your cress seeds why not decorate your shoebox.

Cut your initials in the lid of the shoe box instead of the side of the box, watch your initials grow!

Watch the growth of your seeds carefully and draw pictures and write a diary to record what happens.

What other seeds would you like to grow?

Plant your seeds in soil and feed them with your home made compost (see page 23).

Butterfly Garden

Why we like it

This activity is a long-term project but if you have an area to develop as a butterfly garden you will be able to generate smaller activities around it. In this project you will grow a garden to attract butterflies to feed off the flowers and lay their eggs. You can also link smaller activities to investigate butterflies, moths, bees and mini beasts. A butterfly garden is a great sensory environment.

What you might need

A small garden or patio area
Seeds, seedlings and plants
Some garden tools - trowels
Library books
Wood.

How many can do it

3–15
Try and get members of your community involved also.

Safety Check

Wear gloves and an old jumper when collecting garden material

Be careful around stinging nettles

Where we can do it

The butterfly garden will need to be outside. Have you got an area of garden at your play setting or is there an area in the community you could transform? Ask your local school, contact the council or make a potted garden.
The best position is a sheltered, sunny corner with a wall to allow butterflies to bask in the sunlight and stretch their wings.

How you can do it

1. Design your garden thinking about the needs of butterflies, such as:
Food for adult butterflies—nectar, nectar rich flowers
Food for caterpillars—lots of fresh leaves
Shelter from bad weather
Safe places for eggs and other stages of life cycle
Somewhere to hibernate safely
Butterflies like to visit pink, red and blue flowers such as buddleia, sweet peas and lavender. Sweet smelling flowers are great to attract moths who drink nectar at night (moths can find the flower in the dark by its scent).

2. When planting your seeds or seedlings think about the design of your garden. Is there access for all members of your group? Is the garden going to be colour co-ordinated? If you plant seeds in colour sections each participant could take responsibility for a certain area of the garden. Use lolly sticks to mark and identify each plant. When planting what else do you see? Wood lice, earthworms, spiders and ants are great sources of interest and topics of conversation.

3. Add other features to your garden such as a woodpile to create interest for a variety of minibeasts. The wood pile is a great place for butterflies to hibernate, also a winter haven for queen bumble bees and ladybirds. Go for a walk around your local park or woodland area to collect pieces of wood. Pile the collected wood, leave and watch who comes to visit! Once erected the wood pile must be left undisturbed.

4. What might you plant? To attract butterflies to your garden choose nectar rich varieties such as brambles, buddleia, clover, crab apple, forget-me-not, Helichrysum, honeysuckle, lavender, marguerite, marigold, Michealmas daisy, primrose, ragwort, rosemary, sweet william, thistle and traveller's joy. Plants that will be enjoyed by caterpillars are cabbage, clover, holly, ivy, nasturtium, stinging nettle, thistles and grasses.

5. What butterflies will you see? The most common garden butterflies are Meadow Brown, Large White, Small White, Green-veined White, Brimstone, Orange-tip, Small Skipper, Peacock, Comma and the Gatekeeper. Butterflies migrating to the UK might also visit your summer garden, look out for the Clouded Yellow, Painted Lady and Red Admiral butterflies.

Useful Tips

In a sheltered, sunny patch of your garden introduce stinging nettles. At egg laying time you will see visitors such as the Red Admiral, Peacock, Comma and Small Tortoiseshell. Nettles are a great food source for other insects such as hoverflies, moths and will attract birds.

Spotlight—Lifecycle of a Butterfly

A butterfly has four main stages in its life. The butterfly begins life as an egg and grows into a caterpillar. The caterpillar is the main growing stage and eats lots of leaves. It sheds its skin about four times as it grows. When the caterpillar is fully fed and ready it will form itself into a chrysalis in which the caterpillar's body breaks down into a fluid. The chrysalis remains in its position hanging off a stem or under a leaf until it hatches and a beautiful butterfly will emerge and spread its wings. The adult butterfly feeds from nectar and finds a mate. Some butterflies only live for a few days, others will hibernate or migrate. The butterfly will lay its eggs and the process will begin again for a new life.

Did you know... to tell a butterfly from a day-flying moth, look at the antennae. A butterfly's antennae are knobbed at the top where as a moth's antennae are flat and straight.

Snapshot

Blue Dragon out of school club in Gloucester thoroughly enjoyed their butterfly garden project. The club was able to transform the unused wild garden at the edge of the school field into their very own butterfly garden. The children and playworkers received support from their local community who prepared the wild area so the children could begin planting their garden. The design ensured easy access and easy maintenance. A chequered design with square patio slabs and squares of soil allowed each gardener to look after their own square. They each chose a colour and planted only that colour in their square. While their seeds were growing into healthy flowering plants, the after school club were busy rearing their own butterflies from a butterfly kit (see Caterpillar Houses, page 30). A woodpile was built and a pathway was cleared around the pond and patches of wild grasses and nettles. A child-sized wooden picnic table was donated by a local company.
At the beginning of the summer the butterflies were ready to be released, a party was held in the garden for everyone who had taken part. The club is continuing to maintain their garden with support from the school. All ages thoroughly enjoyed gardening; the younger participants particularly enjoyed finding wood lice and ants.

Useful Tips

Get support from your local community to help you transform a garden area or donate seeds, plants or garden tools.

Borrow books from your local library or look on the Internet to find out more about butterflies, moths and insects. Log on to *www.thebigbugshow.com* for information about insects and bugs. Observe your garden and watch who comes to visit.

Caterpillar Houses

Why we like it?

Rear caterpillars and watch the amazing process of metamorphosis! You can care for and provide a home for caterpillars during their life cycle as they prepare to turn into butterflies. You can construct a caterpillar house and take responsibility for the care of a small number of caterpillars. Buy a 'butterfly kit' if you are in an area with few butterflies. Link this activity to the Butterfly Garden project on page 27.

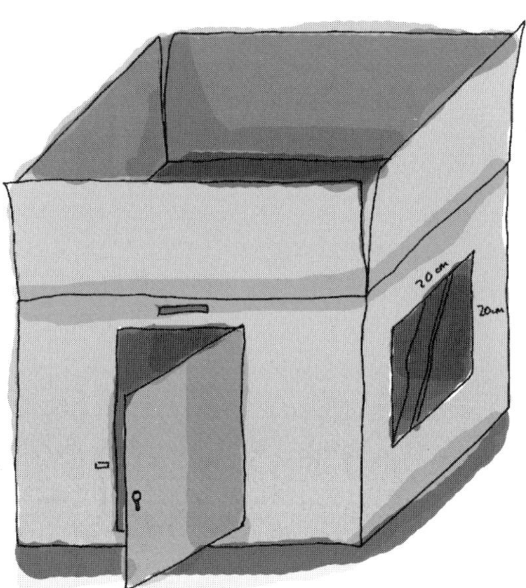

What you might need

A cardboard box approximately 30 cm squared for up to five butterflies. Ask your local shop or supermarket for empty boxes

Some netting

Masking tape or packaging tape

Twine

Newspaper

Scissors and a ruler

A plant suitable for the species of caterpillar or a regular supply of fresh cuttings of your caterpillar's favourite plant

A 'butterfly kit' if you are using one (see page 33).

When and where to do it

The best time of year to start this project is during spring. Plan to release your butterflies into your new garden in early summer. Rearing your butterflies will take about 8 weeks depending on which stage of metamorphosis you start. If housing the caterpillars inside, make sure it is not too warm. Perhaps keep the houses in a shed.

How you can do it

1. Reinforce the base of your box with tape. Cut out three windows and a door in the sides of your box, these will allow you to observe the growing caterpillars. Make your windows about 20 cm x 20 cm. On the fourth side measure a door and mark on the left or right your door hinge. Carefully cut along the three edges of your door—remember not to cut along your door hinge.

2. To keep your box secure you will need a door handle. Cut a slit on the door and one on the wall of your box. Knot pieces of twine through the slits so you can tie the door shut from the outside. Make a handle for your cage too. Cut small slits above the window opposite the door and two slits above the door. Knot a length of twine to the slits.

3. Cut your netting into squares slightly larger than the windows and tape them on the outside of the box. Add a paper towel to the base inside and seal the top of the box with tape. You may wish to decorate your caterpillar house at this stage.

4. Caterpillar search. Many excellent caterpillars can be found by searching plants or bushes in your area during spring and early summer. When you find a caterpillar remove the plant stem it is feeding on and place it gently in a clean and empty jam jar with a lid. Make sure you make a note of the plant your caterpillar was found on and take some stems to put in your caterpillar house. Don't remove lots of caterpillars from one site, the maximum you should take is about five. Alternatively use a 'butterfly kit'.

5. In your caterpillar house you will need to have a supply of the plant the caterpillar was feeding from. The plant needs to be fresh and healthy, caterpillars are fussy eaters. Put stems of the plant in a small pot of water. It is a good idea to stuff cotton wool around the top of the water pot to prevent the caterpillars drowning. Alternatively place a pot plant in your caterpillar house. Gently introduce your caterpillar to its new home. Arrange a couple of twigs to reach the floor of the house so if your caterpillar falls off a twig or stem he can easily climb back up!

6. Spray the inside of your caterpillar house with water very lightly, every day. Avoid large quantities of condensation forming on the inside of the cage, caterpillars can easily drown.

7. As your caterpillar grows he will eat more and more. Make sure you have a good supply of his favourite food.

Spotlight—Caterpillars

Find out more about your caterpillar. Go to your local library and find some books about caterpillars. Can you find out what species your caterpillar is, what sort of butterfly will he turn into? You will watch your caterpillar shed its skin several times and then form itself into a chrysalis where your caterpillar will turn itself into a beautiful butterfly. When your caterpillar is ready to turn into a pupa or chrysalis it will attach itself to a twig or stem. The caterpillar will make a silk thread, which he will use to hold himself to the stem. The chrysalis will look like a leaf when it is complete. The caterpillar is inside the chrysalis and will start to change itself into a butterfly. When he has stopped growing the chrysalis will crack open and a beautiful butterfly will appear.

Useful Tips

Try not to take too many caterpillars from one area.

Feed your caterpillar with fresh food and make sure you find out about your caterpillar's favourite food.

Remember to really look after your caterpillar and be very gentle.

When holding a butterfly, hold it gently at the base of its wings.

The butterfly will need different food such as fresh cut flowers. Perhaps add a small pot with a weak mixture of honey and sugar and give the butterfly a piece of fruit so it can feed on the juices.

Spotlight—Butterfly Kits

If there are not many butterflies in your area you can buy caterpillars to rear. Order a Saver Pack from Worldwide Butterfly. The pack includes 10 Tortoiseshell and 10 Peakcock species. Feed the caterpillars on stinging nettles for four weeks, they will turn into pupae for two weeks and will then hatch. The Saver Pack costs £14.95. Look on the website *www.wwb.co.uk* for more information or call Worldwide Butterflies on 01935 474608.

Insect Lore sell complete butterfly kits. Log on to *www.insectlore-europe.com* to order a catalogue.

What next?

Release your butterflies. Carefully allow the butterflies to leave the caterpillar house. If you need to pick up the butterfly hold it very gently by its body.

Hold a picnic or party for releasing your butterflies in your butterfly garden (see page 27).

Write some poems and short stories about your butterflies.

Continue to observe the butterflies, what are their favourite flowers? Have any butterflies mated? How long do the butterflies live?

Safety Check

Adult help may be necessary when cutting out the windows and door in your caterpillar house

Don't touch caterpillars with your fingers! Caterpillars are very delicate and some species can cause irritation to your skin. Pick up caterpillars on a stem.

Wash your hands after gardening.

Pond Life: Making a Pond in a Box

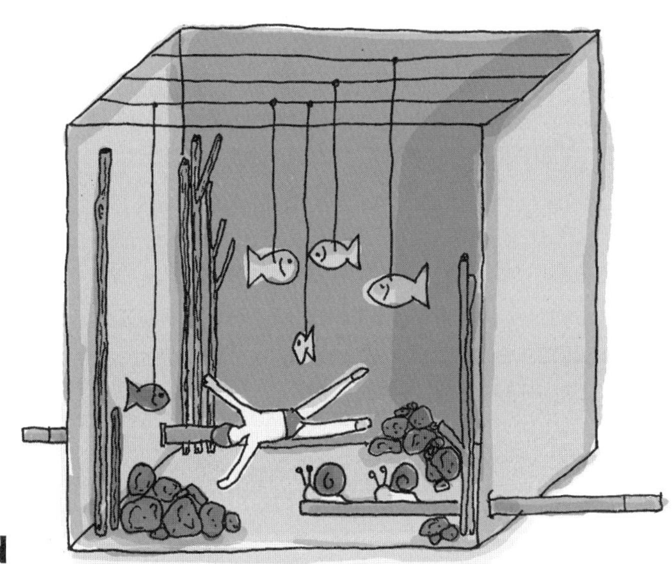

Why we like it

It involves creativity and imagination when making models of fish and other swimming creatures and designing the floor of your pond. You can make your pond life model as simple or detailed as you wish.

What you might need

Cardboard boxes—one each, ask at your local supermarket

Glue

Gaffer tape

A variety of scrap material

A variety of paper, different colours and textures

Crayons

Paints

Cotton thread

Wool or string

Plasticine, clay or blu-tac.

How many can do it

1–15
Work in small groups or make a pond individually.

Where you can do it

Indoors or outdoors on a fine day. Be aware that you will have piles of paper and craft materials.

How you can do it

1. Your cardboard box will be transformed into a pond full of plants and creatures. The top of the box is to be the surface of the pond and in the box is under the water. Carefully cut a window in the side of your box to act as a viewing window.

2. Paint the inside of your box to represent the inside of a pond, experiment with watery painting effects. Stick straws and twigs (using clay, plasticine or blu-tac) to the bottom of the box to make some reeds and pondweed.

3. Make cut-outs and models of fish, frogs, tadpoles, snails and other creatures who live in the pond. Creatures, which crawl along the bottom of the box, can be made from any modelling materials or even painted stones.

4. Attach six or more lengths of cotton thread across the top of your pond. Secure the ends of the thread with sticky tape. Knot another length of thread to one of the horizontal pieces and attach a fish to the end. Let your fish suspend in the pond. Make some pond-skaters, dragonfly and water-boatman and stand them on the horizontal threads so they look as though they are standing on the top of the water.

Safety Check

Ask an adult to help when cutting the cardboard box.

Pond dipping (see below) should be supervised by an adult. Always be careful when playing by the water's edge.

5. Cut out cardboard figures and decorate them so they are 3D. These could be more underwater creatures, human swimmers or a diver, or more mythical creatures such as a mermaid or water monster. Attach the figures to lengths of card with sticky tape. Carefully cut holes in the sides of the box so the puppets can slide in and out, make sure the cardboard handles poke outside the box.

6. Decorate the outside of your box with flowers, plants, grass and animals that might be around your pond.

Snapshot

Pond dipping was such an enjoyed and talked about activity that the children at Bradley's Burrow after school club were pleased by the idea of making pond life models.

Not all the children took part in making a whole pond but everyone joined in making models of stickleback fish, snails and frogs. Making the ponds can take quite a long time so one table was kept as the pond making table for several days. Waiting for paint and glue to dry on the different parts of the model allowed children to join in with other games and activities taking place at the Burrow. A group of three children made a pond together and they created a pondlife puppet theatre. Individual children used smaller cardboard boxes to make their pond scenes. The idea of suspending the fish and other creatures was well received but a little bit fiddly. Karen, the Burrow's volunteer play assistant, stood by to help knot and untangle the thread. After the pond table was cleared up the children presented their ponds to the rest of the club. The puppet theatre trio presented a short play, a story about a tadpole growing into an adult frog, encountering dangers from a cat's paw and hungry fish on the way.

Useful Tips

Do some pond dipping in a local pond to find out what creatures live there.

Use resource books to help identify the creatures.

Ice Sculpting

Why we like it

Playing with water is always a favourite but making an ice sculpture is even more fascinating. There are so many variations to this activity which can appeal to all abilities and interests.

What you might need

Plastic sheets or trays

Rubber gloves

A freezer

PVC Aprons

Pieces of dish cloth

A mop

Water in jugs or supervised use of taps

Clean, empty 1 litre drinks cartons—at least one each

Sculpting tools such as blunt knives and spoons. More experienced ice carvers might be able to use sharper carving tools, providing they are supervised and have practised using them correctly.

For the Ice-lanterns:

A supply of leaves, petals, shells and twigs

Plastic drinks bottles and plastic cups without handles.

For coasters:

Plastic lids from large jars.

How many can do it

1–12.

Where you can do it

It is advisable to make ice sculptures outside, it can be done inside but be prepared for water spills.

How you can do it

1. Carefully cut off the top of a carton. Fill it up with water and place in a freezer. Make sure the carton is stable and will not fall over.

2. Collect twigs, petals, leaves and other materials to use in the other ice activities. While the cartons are freezing make an ice lantern. Using a 2 litre plastic drinks bottle, carefully cut it in half—you may need help from an adult. Take the bottom half of the drinks bottle and tape a plastic cup to the rim of the bottle on two sides (see fig. on page 37). Attach the cup so it is suspended in the middle of the bottle. Drop your leaves, twigs and other pieces into the bottle and fill up with water. To stop the plastic cup from bobbing in the water, place a pebble or ball of plasticine in the cup to weigh it down. Carefully place in the freezer.

3. Once your ice blocks are frozen, cover a table outside with a plastic sheet and put on your aprons.

4. Lift out the frozen cartons from the freezer using rubber gloves or a tea towel. Put your carton on a metal tray and leave to stand for a few minutes. Carefully pull off the carton from the ice. You may need to cut the carton so ask for some help from an adult. If the carton is still stuck place it in a bowl of warm water for a minute or two.

5. Decide what you want to sculpt and begin to chip away the ice with your chosen sculpting tool. Start at the top or on the edges where the ice is less hard.

6. To complete your ice-lantern, take it from the freezer and place in warm water for a couple of minutes. Pour a little warm water in the cup too. Gently wiggle the plastic bottle from the ice and then lift out the cup on top.

7. Put a nightlight candle in the ice lantern and display on a windowsill or outside at the entrance. Display your sculptures on trays on a windowsill so light will shine through them.

8. Hang up your aprons to dry and tidy up the table. Watch how pieces of ice melt back into water. What causes the ice to melt more quickly? Test pieces of ice on your hand and on the ground outside.

Snapshot

Masha is a childminder who introduced her school aged children to ice sculpting during one hot summer week. They made them on the patio table in the yard outside. Masha keeps a close eye on them to guide their technique and reassure them. She often joins in too. The younger children so enjoyed making ice that they continue to try out different moulds such as rubber gloves, plastic bottles and the sandpit toys. Loreen and Murphy, both age 9, created coasters for the children to use one snack time. They used large jar tops, the kind you get from plastic tubs of nuts and raisins, and carefully filled them with water. They sprinkled the water with fallen petals from the fuschia bush and leaves from the mint and parsley plants. The coasters didn't take too long to freeze and looked very pretty. As the ice began to melt Loreen pointed out the smell of mint.

Catherine experimented by holding a torch close to the ice block to speed up the melting process in different parts, the torch wasn't that efficient but it was a good idea and created an interesting effect.

What next?

On a piece of cloth draw a picture in permanent pen or sew on a pattern. Hang the cloth upside down in the carton before the water is frozen taping it to the outside of the carton so it won't move. Your ice block will have a picture inside it.
Make an ice sculpture display for your parents and friends to come and see.

Useful Tips

When ice sculpting do it on a tray to catch any melting water. Stand the ice block on a dishcloth to prevent it from sliding.

Prepare the cartons in a previous session and think about what you might like to sculpt before hand.

Safety Check

Adult supervision is required for much of this activity—from using tools, to ensuring that gloves or a tea towel are used when removing ice from the freezer.

When sculpting be very careful not to jab your hand or anyone else's.

If you do spill water or your sculptures begin to melt, mop up straight away.

Don't touch ice straight out of the freezer with your bare hands.

When chipping the ice, do it away from your body and ensure correct use of tools.

Don't touch anything electrical with wet hands.

Magic Mosaics

Why we like it

It is easy to do and produces fantastic results. A mosaic is a beautiful creation, you can keep it for years. You can design a mosaic as a sign or logo or something more individual. Mosaic making requires concentration and an eye for colour, pattern and design.

What you might need

Base card, wood or plastic (to a manageable size for your mosaic)

Bag of tile grout

Old pottery or small tiles

Shells, beads, marbles (optional)

A sheet or box

Gardening gloves

Spatula

Goggles.

How many can do it

2–10.

Where you can do it

Outdoors or indoors.

Safety Check

Wear goggles and gloves when breaking tiles and have adult supervision.

Always wear gloves when handling broken pieces.

Wash your hands after grouting and wear an apron.

Adult supervision required.

How you can do it

1. Collect together a variety of old pottery of varied colours. Has your local scrap store got some interesting tiles? Visit charity shops or ask at a pottery outlet for any redundant pottery. Also consider glass pebbles, terracotta pieces and plastic tiles.

2. Design your mosaic. Keep the picture or pattern simple and think about the use of colour.

3. Draw an outline of the picture or pattern on the base card or wood. Highlight sections and colour requirements. Draw the same onto a piece of paper.

4. Prepare your mosaic tiles. If you haven't already got small pieces its time to get smashing! Collect a few pieces of pottery and lay carefully inside a sheet. Put on your goggles and wrap up the sheet. Using a wooden mallet, hit the pottery through the sheet. Alternatively put the pottery into a cardboard box, seal the box securely and shake it to break the pieces. An adult should supervise or assist with the smashing.

5. Empty the pieces called 'tesserae' onto sheets of newspaper. Wearing gloves pick out the best pieces. Wrap up the paper and throw the rest away. Sweep up any pieces or shards of pottery.

6. Sort the mosaic pieces into different colours.

7. Mix up the tile grouting with water (see packet instructions). Cover the base of your mosaic with the grouting.

8. Lay the 'tesserae' or pottery pieces onto the grouting. Leave a space between each tesserae. Use the design you drew on the paper to guide you. Lay each piece before the grouting dries.

9. Once all the tesserae are laid, add more grouting over the top so it fills the gaps. Carefully wipe off surplus grouting and leave to dry.

10. With a damp cloth wipe over the mosaic to remove the grouting from the surface of the tiles.

11. If holes in the grouting appear rub in dry grouting, when settled wipe over the surface again.

12. Display your mosaic with pride.

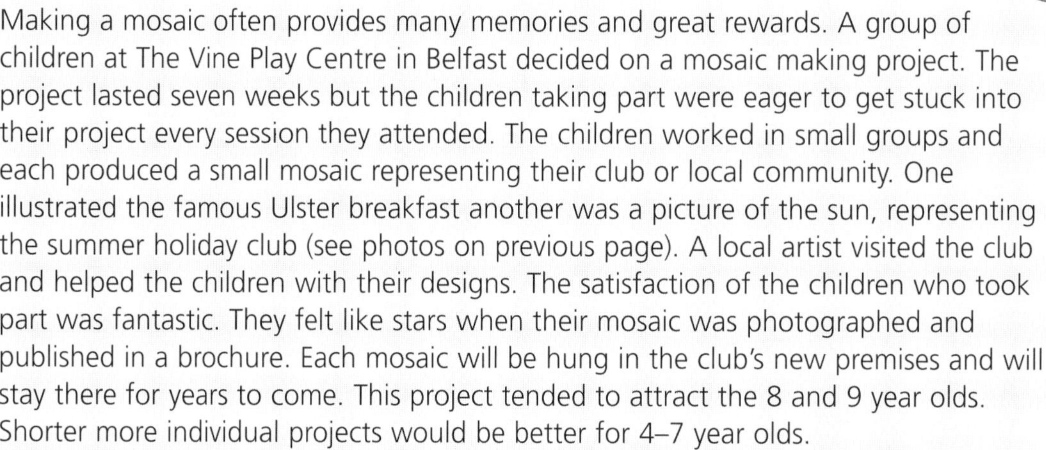

Snapshot

Making a mosaic often provides many memories and great rewards. A group of children at The Vine Play Centre in Belfast decided on a mosaic making project. The project lasted seven weeks but the children taking part were eager to get stuck into their project every session they attended. The children worked in small groups and each produced a small mosaic representing their club or local community. One illustrated the famous Ulster breakfast another was a picture of the sun, representing the summer holiday club (see photos on previous page). A local artist visited the club and helped the children with their designs. The satisfaction of the children who took part was fantastic. They felt like stars when their mosaic was photographed and published in a brochure. Each mosaic will be hung in the club's new premises and will stay there for years to come. This project tended to attract the 8 and 9 year olds. Shorter more individual projects would be better for 4–7 year olds.

What next?

Follow the project with smaller mosaic activities such as mosaic mirrors. Attach mosaic shells, beads or tiles to the edges of a mirror to frame it using the mosaic making technique above.

Make mosaic coasters. You can use old square coasters and revamp them into funky mosaic creations.

Ask a local artist or an Arts Initiative to work with you or provide ideas and tips. Library books could provide helpful tips and creative ideas such as *Tiling and Mosaics* by Deena Beverley, published in 1999 by Merehurst, London.

Spotlight—An Ancient Art

Invented by the Greeks, the art of mosaics has been practised for thousands of years. In the Roman city of Pompeii in Italy, mosaics survive. On occasions, Romans decorated their pavements with marble mosaics!

Useful Tips

If you are making a large mosaic don't cover the whole surface in grouting, it may dry before you are finished.

In your design, create straight lines to distinguish the pattern. For example where the tiles change colour to illustrate an object, keep the outside line of the object straight so it appears clear.

If you are unsure about smashing pottery or tiles use beads, shells, stones, glass pebbles or pieces of plastic to make your mosaic.

Buy a mosaic set which will include ready to use tesserae. Mosaic kits are available in most crafts shops, toy shops and department stores.

Music from Junk

Why we like it

Everyone can join in making music whether it is creating a rhythm, playing a melody or creating unusual sounds. Making your own instruments is even better as you realise how the instrument makes sound. It encourages concentration, co-ordination and listening hard. Look out for the range of instruments made in other countries and try to recreate some of the techniques used to make them. Reuse household objects and rubbish to create a percussion band.

What you might need

A large plastic bowl
A balloon
Scissors
Plastic bottles or yoghurt pots or boxes
Rice, sand, pebbles or beads
Jam jars
Pieces of chiffon or another soft material
A stick
Plastic washing up bowl and bucket
A dustbin lid
Wooden spoons
An empty tissue box
Thick elastic bands
Cardboard tubes
Metal spoons
Saucepan lids
Cardboard tubing
A small sheet of sandpaper
Two bath sponges.

How many can do it

2–25
A group of 4–8 is a good number to make a percussion band.

Where you can do it

Make your instruments indoors but on a fine day play your music outdoors. Small rooms or areas for children to practice their instrument are useful.

How you can do it

1. Display all your materials on a table and think about the different ways you can make music from them. How can a washing up bowl and washing up brush make music? Bang, crash, scrape, rattle and shake are the methods of playing percussion instruments.

All the materials on your table will make some kind of sound but pick out the sounds which could be used to make music. Instruments you could make are drums, cymbals, maracas and jarophones.

2. Any hollow tin or box can be used as a drum. Strike it with a stick like beater. Turn over a washing up bowl and hit it with a washing up brush to make an interesting sound.

Make a drainpipe drum by stretching brown tape over one end of the pipe. Overlap the pieces of tape and wrap some around the side of the pipe. Hold the drum under your arm and tap the taped end with your fingers. Cut a balloon in half and stretch it over a large plastic bowl. Ask someone to hold the balloon in place while you tape the balloon securely to the bowl. This is a tub drum, strike it with a wooden stick.

3. Make some maracas by pouring some rice, beans or lentils into two dry plastic bottles. Screw the tops on securely. Decorate the bottles with coloured paper and give them a shake.

4. Make a South American vihuela or small guitar out of a tissue box. Stretch 4 or 5 thick elastic bands over the box in rest them over the centre of the opening with at least 1 cm between each elastic band. Snip the end of a cardboard tube so the flaps can be bent outwards and tape the tube to the side of the box to act as a guitar arm.

5. To make a jaraphone, line up four jam jars and fill each one with a different amount of water. Cut out four pieces of chiffon and cover each jam jar. The material needs to be pulled taught across each jar. Secure it with an elastic band or tie it with some string. If you use tape it needs to be strong like gaffer tape. Use a handle of a wooden spoon to strike the material. Line up the jars in order of the notes they produce.

6. Two saucepan lids, of the same size, held by the handles will make good cymbals. Clash them together and as soon as they impact quickly pull them apart in a dramatic gesture.

7. Glue a piece of sandpaper onto two bath sponges or blocks of wood. Once the glue is dry, hold the sponges so the sand-papered sides are facing and rub them together. This is a quiet version of shuffle boards.

What next?

Make a cluster drum with a variety of lengths of drainpipe. With the heads of the drums level tape all the drums together in a cluster. Twist the tape around one pipe and join on to another, twist tape around that pipe and join on to another and so on. Make interesting rhythms with your drum.

Find out about other instruments from books or a visit to a music shop.

Invite a musician to visit your playsetting and help you create your own music.

Get together and make a percussion band with the instruments above and any others you can come up with.

Make sound affects for stories or plays. Record these on a tape-recorder.

Bring in your own instruments such as recorders and ask the percussion band to accompany you.

Sit down in a circle and play the silence game. Begin by being quiet, and then become really, really quiet. Listen to the silence, what do you hear? Sound will start to emerge from the silence such as gurgles from the radiator or even gurgles from somebody's tummy. What sounds can you hear from outside? End silence by recalling what sounds you heard.

Look at music activity books such as *Music For Everyone: a guide for playworkers in out of school clubs*, published by the London Mozart Players in conjunction with Kids' Clubs Network. This guide is an ideal for resource for childcare groups. Mail order only from Kids' Clubs Network, call 020 7512 2112 for an order form.

Useful Tips

When striking your drums, let the drum-head ring.
Set up a row of different drums in front of you, like a drum kit, so you can make a rhythm using different tones.
Use the jarophone to make a melody or include an instrument such as a recorder or keyboard.
Dance around when playing the maracas or tambourine and play the cymbals dramatically.
Remember that your body can be a musical instrument—clap your hands, stamp your feet, whistle and hum.
Use your instruments to accompany one of your favourite songs to sing.

Making Paper

Why we like it

This activity demonstrates how paper is made. It also introduces recycling and the idea of making new from old. All ages and abilities can take part from tearing up paper to squashing soggy paper to a pulp and making paper moulds. The more confident and adventurous participants can get creative with dyes and textures.

What you might need

Used paper: envelopes, paper bags and computer paper

A square of thin wire mesh or wire coat hanger and a pair of thin tights

Hand towels or dish cloths

A heavy weight such as a book or brick

Scissors

Elastic band or piece of string

A large bucket

A plastic bowl

Water

A blunt knife

Long, thick piece of wood

Electric liquidiser or whisk (optional).

Where to do it

This can be done indoors or outside. Perhaps make the paper pulp outdoors. You will need an indoor area for drying paper and some where to soak paper overnight.

How many can do it

Ideally 2–4 in a group.
Each coat hanger mould will make one sheet of paper in each session. For a larger group you will need more bowls and buckets.

Useful Tips

Remember not to pour pulp down the drain! Drain the water from the pulp through a sieve or fine mesh.

How you can do it

1. Begin by investigating what paper is made from. If you tear a piece of newspaper you will notice tiny hairs, these are the plant fibres which all paper is made from.

2. Collect old paper and tear it into small strips. Fill a bucket with warm water and add the torn pieces of paper. The paper will need to soak overnight, be careful when moving the full buckets and store somewhere safe.

3. Make a paper mould out of a wire coat hanger and some tights. Cut off a leg from a pair of tights and knot the toe. Slide your hanger inside the tights and down to the knot. Holding the hook gently pull down the hanger to bend the wire into a square. Knot the tights at the hook with the hook uncovered. Cut off the excess. Alternatively, use a square of thin wire mesh.

4. Pour away the water from the bucket. Refill the bucket half full with fresh water Using a wooden stick stir, mash and beat the soaked paper. Use a hand whisk to create a pulp. The consistency should be smooth and creamy and it may take a bit of time to achieve this. Use a liquidiser to speed up the process—put mixture in the jug and add water until it is three-quarters full. Liquidise batches in short bursts until the paper turns into white pulp.

5. Half fill your plastic bowl with water and pour in the paper pulp. Stir the pulp thoroughly with the water, get rid of as many lumps as possible.

6. Hold your paper mould by the hook and submerge it into the pulp sideways so a thin layer forms on the top. Hold the mould flat in the mixture and lift it up out of the pulp. Let the water drain through the mesh.

7. Gently shake the paper mould to help the fibres settle.

8. Press the mould or mess pulp down onto the towel. Press hard and then peel the mould or mesh off to leave an even layer of pulp on the towel.

9. Lay another towel on top and add another layer of pulp, carry on until you run out of pulp and towels.

10. Put a heavy weight on top of the last towel and leave to dry overnight.

11. Remove each towel layer and careful lift off the pressed paper.

What next?

Add colour to your paper by adding a mug of tea or pieces of coloured paper to your pulp. Mix powder paint with a little water and add to your pulp for brighter colours. Try natural colourings.

Add glitter, pressed flowers, flower petals, cotton or wool to create unusual textures.

Experiment with different types of paper and make different pulp consistencies.

You will notice that your paper is very fibrous and has a lot of texture. Think about how you are going to use your hand made paper.

Draw or paint pictures of trees and the animals which live around the trees.

Make greetings cards and envelopes out of your paper.

Spotlight—Reducing Waste Paper

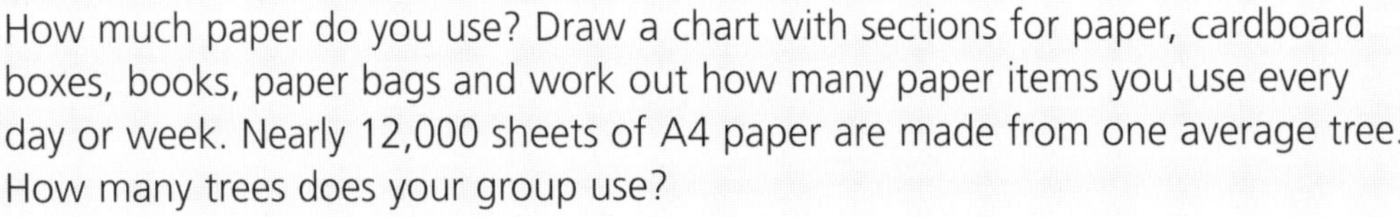

How much paper do you use? Draw a chart with sections for paper, cardboard boxes, books, paper bags and work out how many paper items you use every day or week. Nearly 12,000 sheets of A4 paper are made from one average tree. How many trees does your group use?

Safety Check

An adult should supervise use of the liquidiser.

Be careful with the wire coat hangers; if you are concerned about the wire hooks cover them with tape.

Wear an apron when pulping the soggy paper. Clear up any spills on the floor straight away to prevent any accidents.

Sparkle Paper

Why we like it

This activity is brilliant because you can work with a large group and it is a quick creative activity. All children of all abilities can take part. You will transform blank tissue paper into beautiful sheets of hand made decorative paper to use for wall decorations, window pictures or special wrapping paper. Visit a scrap store for materials. This can be a quick creative activity requiring very little adult supervision.

What you might need

Sheets of plastic such as plastic folders or builders plastic

Multiple sheets of tissue paper

A range of sequins, feathers, ribbons, string and other sparkly materials

PVA glue and glue brushes

Paint brushes

Aprons

Area for drying paper over night.

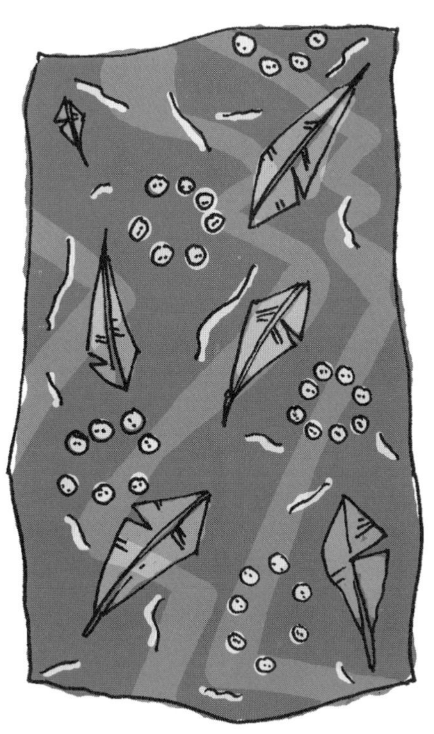

Where you can do it

You will need a large flat surface and somewhere easy to sweep up afterwards. Recommended indoors.

How many can do it

1–15 depending on space and materials.

How you can do it

1. Gather a good array of materials. A great place to do that is at your local scrap store or contact a clothes manufacturer or a haberdashery near you for any off cuts and donations of materials.

2. On your flat surface lay out the different materials in containers in the centre of your area, easily accessibly for all participants. Each participant must have a sheet of plastic as a base. Lay the first sheet of tissue paper on the plastic sheet. Make sure the plastic sheet is slightly larger than the tissue paper sheet.

3. How are you going to design your sparkle paper and how will you get the best results? Which colours of tissue paper are you going to use and which materials are you going to glue in? If you are going to use the sparkle paper as wrapping paper think about the person you are giving it to—what is their favourite colour?

4. Paint the first sheet of tissue paper with a layer of glue. Arrange a variety of sequins and materials on that sheet. Take a new sheet of tissue paper and carefully lay it on top. You can also rip up sheets of tissue paper and lay different colours and shapes. Make sure you cover the sheet completely, don't leave any holes! You could also make a creative texture by scrunching pieces of tissue paper. Allow this first layer to dry for a few minutes and then repeat the process of painting on glue and adding the sparkly materials. Continue layering until you are ready. We suggest using 3 layers.

5. Let your snazzy paper fully dry to prevent damage and for the sparkly bits to stick. A natural break to play a game or have a snack! If it is a fine day perhaps lay your sheets outside and put pebbles on the overlapping plastic. Do not remove the plastic at this stage. It is likely that the paper will need to dry overnight. Perhaps set up a washing line in a quiet room.

6. The next session you can look forward to seeing your hand made sparkly paper when dry and it will look very different. Carefully peel off the plastic sheet from your paper. Hold your new sheet up to the light and it should sparkle. Sign your name in one of the corners of the paper.

7. There are many ways to display your paper. It will be excellent as a window picture and will diffuse coloured light into your setting.

Useful Tips

Each layer must have a complete covering of tissue paper—make sure there are no holes.

Mix PVA glue with water to a thin consistency.

Use wide soft glue brushes—so you don't have to apply too much pressure on delicate paper.

Have paints available too. The best materials to use are feathers, leaves, sequins and pieces of string.

Snapshot

This activity has been popular at a playscheme in East London, for making Diwali cards. The children were eager to use their hand-made sparkle paper. Neeraj's father had given the playscheme a bag full of colourful sequins, and the children all found them perfect for decorating their sparkle paper for their cards. The results were brilliant!

What next?

Making sparkly paper can effectively be two activities. One session you will make the paper the next session you will make something with the dried paper. The drying time needed is the only catch. Make sure you have a game or plenty of other play opportunities to move on to once the paper been made!

Decorate your display board with your new paper to make a colourful sight and impress your visitors.

Tape the sparkle paper to a window and enjoy the coloured light shining through. Does your paper sparkle in the sun?

Use your sparkly paper as special wrapping paper for a present or make a card.

Draw a picture or paint on the sparkly paper, be careful what art materials you use so not to rip the paper.

Write a story or poem and present it on the sparkle paper. Decorate the paper with items that appear in a story.

You can change the type of material you use in your paper. Perhaps follow an environmental theme and use feathers, leaves, petals. Make sure the materials you glue inside your paper are lightweight.

Safety Check

Be aware of the temptation to put beads, sequins and other small materials in mouths, ears or noses!

Recyclesaurus

Why we like it

With the ever-increasing amount of rubbish we create, the 'Recyclesaurus' would be a welcome friend! This rubbish eating dinosaur comes to life in the form of a collage. You can use your imagination in collecting materials for the collage and practising your creative talents when making it. As the dinosaur comes to life you may become absorbed into his world of recycling. What would life be like with Recyclesaurus around?

What you might need

Large sheet of cardboard 183 cm x 125 cm

Lots of old newspaper

PVA glue and brushes

Flour and water

Kitchen roll or tissue paper

Paper and polystyrene cartons

Pumpkins seeds

Assorted material

Garden tags

Variety of scrap store and recycled materials.

How many can do it

2–20.

Where you can do it

Indoors.

Useful Tips

Use items that you regularly throw away such as toothpaste boxes, paper bags, plastic bottle tops, magazines and polystyrene fillings.

Fill the dinosaur's tummy with food (recycled materials!)

Use foil and shiny materials to create effects.

Add horns on the dinosaur's head like a Triceratops, Recyclesaurus could use the horns to pick up litter.

Bone plates, like those on the back and tail of a Stegosaurus could be used to store cans and cartons. Make them out of painted corrugated card.

Use garden tags to create teeth, a marble for the eye, or pumpkin seeds, buttons and bottle tops to decorate the face.

How you can do it

1. Lay out your base material, sheet of paper or card and arrange an area for your collection of materials.

2. Draw an outline of your dinosaur and any other features you would like to include such as a background landscape. Make your dinosaur as big as possible to create a fantastic effect.

3. Be creative and imaginative with your collage and think about how best to use your recycled materials. Why not make your dinosaur 3D by using an old sheet as the dinosaur's skin and stuffing the inside with paper, fabric or old material. Tuck in any extra fabric and secure the sheet to the shape of the dinosaur template using tape and glue. Or, make the body of the dinosaur by scrunching up balls of newspaper. Brush the balls with PVA glue and stick to the base cardboard.

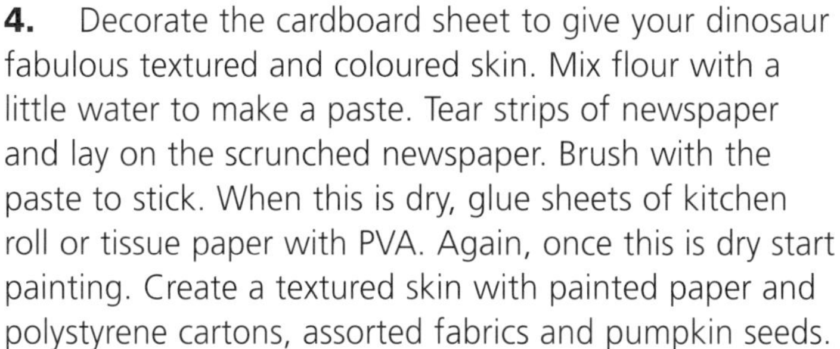

4. Decorate the cardboard sheet to give your dinosaur fabulous textured and coloured skin. Mix flour with a little water to make a paste. Tear strips of newspaper and lay on the scrunched newspaper. Brush with the paste to stick. When this is dry, glue sheets of kitchen roll or tissue paper with PVA. Again, once this is dry start painting. Create a textured skin with painted paper and polystyrene cartons, assorted fabrics and pumpkin seeds.

5. Create an imaginative background on the collage.

6. Make a banner to title your collage.

7. Develop a life for your Recyclesaurus: what is his favourite food—yesterday's newspaper or plastic bottles? What is his favourite hobby and where does he live?

8. When your collage is dry display the picture on the wall of your play setting.

9. Make a frame out of recycled materials to finish it off.

 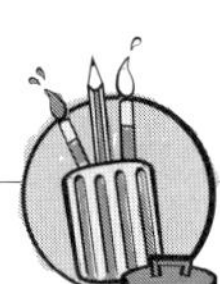

Snapshot

Munching and crunching on rubbish thrown away, boxes and cartons, bottles and cans fill my tummy each day. This is the story of a Welsh Recyclesaurus. The children had a brilliant time creating their dino-collage. Although the idea of a collage was suggested by the playleader, how it was developed was totally up to the children. The recycling dinosaur was decided because the group already had an interest in dinosaurs and reusing materials. In preparation the children decided to tie-dye an old sheet to use as the body of their creature. Sharon wanted the dinosaur to have a textured skin and the white circles in the tie-dye gave the textured effect she imagined. The group collected old newspapers and magazine from friends and neighbours and the dentist and doctor's waiting rooms, and stuffed their dinosaur to fill up his tummy. Blue plastic was glued to create a lake. As 'Recyclesaurus' was being made the children talked about what he would eat and where he liked to go—sticking to the theme of recycling and the re-use of everyday materials. Jack and Matthew dressed themselves as dinosaurs using extra collage material. The group has adapted their favourite game 'What's the time Mr Wolf' to a dinosaur theme. The dinosaur (Mr Wolf) wears a head-dress Jon and Katie made and the children enjoy running away and squawking as if they are Pterodactyls.

What next?

Write a story about your Recyclesaurus.

Create another dinosaur with another theme.

Extend play opportunities around dinosaurs—can you re-create a dinosaur landscape to play in? Or a miniature one in the sandpit?

Make dinosaur masks.

Make a chicken wire Recyclesaurus to stand outside. Encourage parents and other members of the local community to recycle cans, bottles and newspapers.

Safety Check

An adult should check all recycled materials for safety.

Wash hands after handling recycled materials.

Sweep the floor regularly of any scraps of paper or material.

Recycle and Reuse—Cut Down on your Rubbish

Why we like it

This activity focuses on what we throw away and provides a new perspective on each item of 'rubbish'. All ages will enjoy this game and everyone can have a go. All children enjoy play opportunities which appeal to their senses. You will rely on touch alone to find out what is in the mystery rubbish bag.

What you might need

A sack, paper bag or box

A variety of 'safe' household rubbish items, including a few items such as a wet teabag, a wrinkly carrot or potato

A blindfold such as a soft scarf.

Safety Check

Wash your hands after touching the rubbish. Don't use sharp objects such as opened tins or dangerous objects such as bleach bottles.

How many can do it

2–10

Play this game in small groups so everyone is interested and involved.

Where you can do it

A great game to play outdoors but also suitable for indoor play.

How you can do it

1. Fill the sack or box with clean and safe pieces of rubbish, out of view from the people taking part.

2. Gather around the box whether on the table or on the ground.

3. Blindfold the first volunteer who will put his or her hand into the box a pick out a piece of rubbish. From touch alone the volunteer must guess what it is. Remove the blindfold and see whether your guess was correct. Was it easy or hard to guess?

4. Each participant is blindfolded in turn and pick and item of rubbish. Carry on until you have removed all the rubbish from the box.

5. Think about the rubbish you have touched, was the bin the right place for the rubbish or could it have been dealt with in another way (for example put in a compost heap, put in a recycling bin or used for craft activities)?

6. Wash your hands when you have finished the game.

Snapshot

Outside a community centre in East London the children often pass piles of full black plastic bags waiting to be taken to the landfill site. The childcare group played the blindfold game one afternoon and decided to use recycling and rubbish as a theme for their activities for the week. Due to the varying interests of the children a wide range of games and activities took place. Some children drew pictures of the rubbish they see regularly and made up slogans to stop people from dropping litter. The group displayed these on the information board at the front of the community centre. Karin and Bina wrote a letter to their local MP asking for more recycling bins. Aran wrote a poem about rubbish in English and Naomi helped him translated it into Bangladeshi. They made a collage out of pieces rubbish and displayed the poems on the collage. The older boys Jack and Sam designed and made flyers for the residents who live near the community centre. Accompanied by their playleader they delivered their flyers asking residents to not drop litter, to recycle cans and paper and keep the area around the community centre clean and rubbish free. During snack time the children discussed the problems with rubbish and why they want rubbish free streets.

What next?

How can you reduce the amount of rubbish in your bin? Think more about recycling activities.

Take a look at the Recycalsaurus activity on page 52.

Look at what materials will rot in a compost heap. Eggshells, cardboard, leaves and banana skins will rot in a compost but old food tins, fish fingers, chips and bread crusts will not.

Make your own compost maker, turn to page 23.

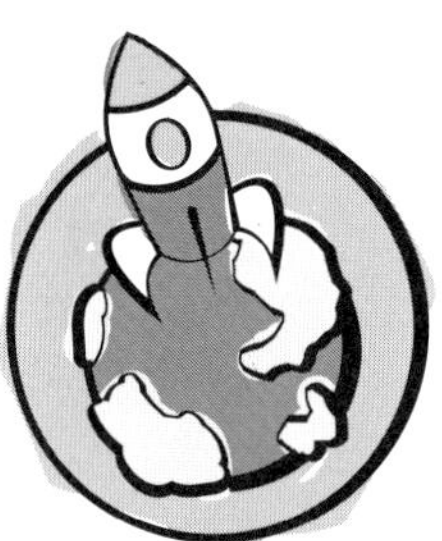

Rocket Journey

Why we like it

It can fuel your imagination with thoughts of whizzing through space. The rocket journey is achievable for everybody providing there is access for everyone to get inside the rocket. The rocket journey provides a focus for collective play or a quiet area for individuals. It can be a great sensory environment and provide lots of play opportunities.

What you might need

Six pieces of corrugated cardboard approximately 150 cm in length and 60 cm wide

Several large pieces of corrugated cardboard, ask at your local supermarket for large cardboard boxes.

Smaller pieces of thin cardboard

Recycled materials

Velcro strips

Poster paints

Silver materials such as foil, sequins and stickers

Black card

Pens and pencils, crayons or chalk

Tape recorder

Favourite rocket or space story.

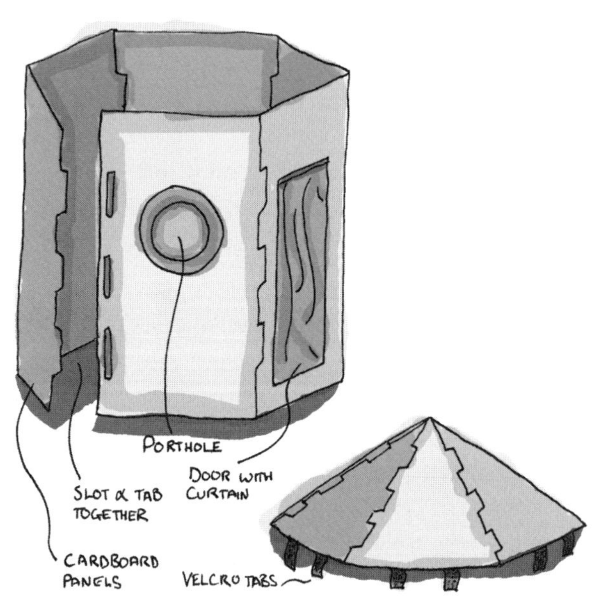

How many can do it?

3–7.

Where to do it

Find a quiet corner to house your rocket, near an electrical socket point.

How you can do it

1. Use the corrugated cardboard to construct the body of the rocket. To join the sides and to make the rocket sturdy cut tabs and slots to fix each edge together. Slat together each piece to make a hexagonal shape. Add packaging tape to secure the sides further. Stand up the rocket body.

2. Carefully cut out a doorway and attach a piece of grey or silver fabric to act as a curtain.

3. The top of the rocket is made out of triangle shapes. Cut out six triangles each with a base length the same as the width of each side, for example 60 cm. Leave extra cardboard on the sides of the triangles to use to cut tabs to slat the triangles together. Attach the top to the main body using velcro pads.

4. Draw portholes on the sides of the rocket inside and out. Decorate the windows to illustrate what you might see out of a rocket porthole when travelling through space. To achieve a view of stars and planets stick lots of silver glitter and stars to one side of a piece of transparent paper with PVA glue. Lay another piece of transparent paper on top and hang up to dry.

5. Cut out the portholes in the sides of the rocket, you may need help with this. Once the paper is dry cut it to shape and attach it to the portholes. Attach small sheets of silver foil or paper to the inside of the portholes to act as curtains.

6. Paint the rocket with silver paint or whatever colour you imagine your rocket should be, adding any graphics or extra pieces of equipment such as a camera, rocket launcher, a weather detector and an antenna.

7. Decorate the inside of the rocket with pictures of the technical apparatus used to fly the rocket, information about the planets, asteroids and the sun. What else would you expect to see inside your rocket?

8. Have you got a favourite story about space travel? If not, why not write a story about travelling in space. Make up some sound effects. Find a quiet space and read out your story and the sound affects, recording it on a tape recorder.

9. Position your rocket close to a plug point so your tape recorder can reach inside the space-craft. Make a seat out of a sturdy box such as a plastic storage box and secure a pillow or cushion on top. Put the tape recorder under the seat and travel into space with your story tape.

Useful Tips

Alternative porthole material could be netting, black or blue paper painted with bright stars, rockets and planets. On the outside of the rocket why not paint faces of astronauts looking out of the rocket.

Wait for the paint and glue to dry before embarking on your rocket journey.

Try and keep the area around the rocket reasonably quiet to enhance the experience of the journey.

Don't let the rocket get over-crowded.

Safety Check

Adult assistance will be needed for cutting out the portholes and doorway.

Cover up any leads from the tape recorder and remember to unplug when you are finished.

Snapshot

Rollercoasters play centre found this to be a very inclusive activity. Painting the rocket vertically was difficult for the children in wheelchairs, so they used mini rollers attached to cardboard tubes enabling the children to dip into the trays of paint and paint the sides of the rocket. The rocket has been used for children to sit alone, relax and talk quietly. The rocket journey has been really popular as the children love to hear themselves on the tape and join in with the sound effects. The decoration inside the rocket has provided a brilliant sensory environment with lots of things to touch, hear, see and imagine.

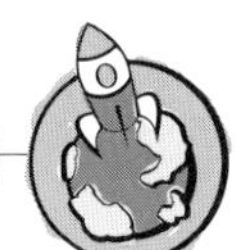

Elephant Adventures

Why we like it

The elephant is an interesting animal and a gigantic theme for many activities whether you choose to dress up, paint or model elephants or use them to discover different countries. Elephant adventures can be adapted for all ages and abilities providing imaginative play opportunities and group games. Elephants can encourage communication.

What you might need

For the mask making you will need materials such as paper plates, cardboard tubes from kitchen rolls, PVA glue, string or elastic, scissors and grey paint.

For Elephants Never Forget you will need 10–20 items such as a bunch of keys, a banana, a leaf, a sweet, a badge and so on, a tea towel and a tray.

For the pop up card in 'What next?' you will 2 sheets of white paper or card per person and coloured pencils or crayons.

How many can do it

1–20
(At least six players for the Elephant, Palm Tree, Giraffe game).

Where to do it

Indoor or outdoors. The games are easy to play outside.

How you can do it

1. Begin by getting into character. Think about the main features of elephants—the long trunk, sounds they use to communicate, the herd walking in single file, flapping big ears and trumpeting noises when approached by lions.

2. Make an elephant mask. Hold a paper plate up to your face and mark where your eyes are. Cut two small holes at these marks and snip a hole either side of the plate to attach a piece of string or elastic.

3. Tape a 30 cm long cardboard tube, for example a kitchen roll tube, to the middle of the mask, this will be the trunk. Halfway up the tube, about 12 cm from the plate make a cut in the tube. This enables the trunk to bend.

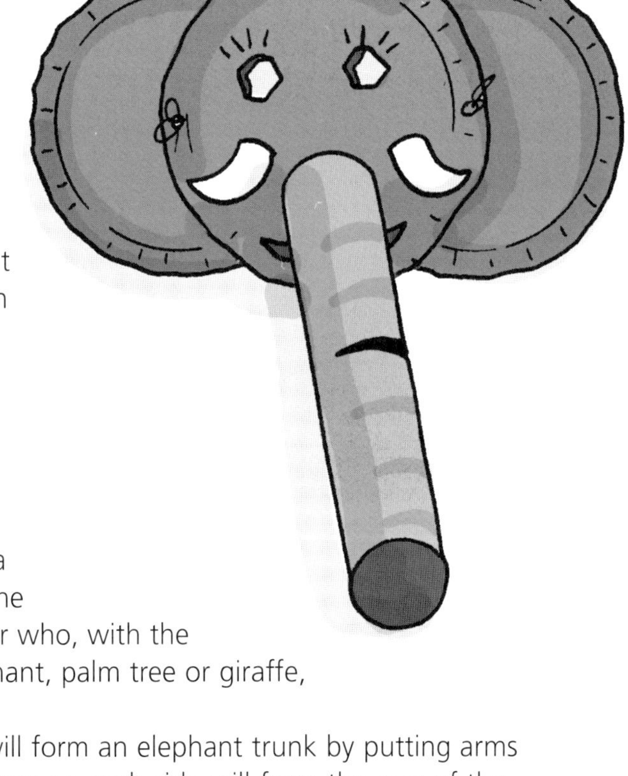

4. Cut a paper plate in half and tape each half to the back sides of the mask so the curved edges appear as if ears. Paint the front of the mask with grey paint. Paint or draw on features such as a lower lip, tusks and eye lashes.

5. Put on your masks and get into character again.

6. Play Elephant, Palm Tree, Giraffe. Form a circle with one person in the middle who is the teller. The middle person will point to a player who, with the players either side, will have to form an elephant, palm tree or giraffe, depending on what the teller calls.
If 'elephant' is called out the chosen player will form an elephant trunk by putting arms straight in front crossed at the wrists. The player on each side will form the ears of the elephant by bending toward and cupping around their mouths with their hands as if whispering to the picked player.

If 'giraffe' is called out the chosen player should raise and extend her arms above her head with fingers closed. The side players to grab her waist bending over.

The third call is 'palm tree'. If you are chosen you must raise your arms above your head in 'Y' formation, fingers open. Side players do the same but lean outwards, away from you.

Useful Tips

The object of the Elephant, Palm Tree, Giraffe game is to try to keep changing all the time. The game has to be played quickly. As soon as an object is formed, the teller has to point to another player. A lively game involving co-ordination, teamwork and quick responses.

7. Play Elephants Never Forget. Lay 10 to 20 items on a tray and cover with a cloth. The elephants should sit around the tray with some paper, pens and pencils. Lift off the cloth, make sure everyone can see the tray, and allow 30 seconds for the elephants to observe the tray. Cover again with the cloth. Elephants must remember as many items and record them by drawing or writing them down. After a few minutes join together and see how many you could remember.

Spotlight—Elephants

Today, only African and Asian elephants survive. African elephants are the largest land animals in the world, imagine the weight of six family cars, this is the weight of an adult African elephant. Despite its size the elephant is a gentle and intelligent giant. Elephants live in family groups and the herd often walks in single file in search of food and water. Elephants are vegetarians and eat 200 kilograms of food a day. The elephant's trunk is a nose and upper lip. They use it like a hand reaching for branches and fruit and use it to suck up water. To prevent overheating elephants either stand under the shelter of trees or submerge themselves in water and mud. They are good swimmers and use their trunks as a snorkel. Elephants communicate with different sounds—trumpets, growls, snorts and deep stomach rumblings that can travel miles. They hold out their huge ears to catch distant sounds. Elephants can live for sixty years and have excellent memories. The leader of the herd, the matriarch, has a great knowledge of the places to find food and water, how best to avoid predators and keep the family safe. Elephants can find safety in National Parks and Reserves.

Snapshot

Karen brought her book on elephants to the Kingfisher Play Club. The children were curious about elephants so elephants were the main theme of the afternoon. While talking about the characteristics of elephants and the different facts each child knew the group made elephant masks. Karen, Trudy, Aaron and Lenny rushed out into the garden to play 'elephants'. They used their arms to act as tails and stomped around as a herd. Imagining the herd had travelled to a lake, the children lifted their trunks to spray water over one another. Karen took on the role as the matriarch and enjoyed screeching and flapping her ears whenever danger prevailed such as Gareth pretending to stalk them as a tiger.

Everyone joined in with the Elephant, Palm Tree, Giraffe game and sat outside on the grass. Playworker Sandra was the teller and used sign language as well as the call. Grant and Ashu are profoundly deaf but the group are good at adapting games to be as inclusive as possible. It is also more interesting for the other children who are learning sign language when they play. The children thoroughly enjoyed the game. They had to think and react quickly, use co-ordination and work together.

The children were still interested in elephants and developed the theme in different ways. A small group wanted to make cards so they enjoyed making the pop-up elephant card. Karen and Jessica went back to the book and made drawings and stories. Another group played Elephants Never Forget and exercised their memory skills.

What next?

Collect and read stories about elephants.

Make a pop-up card. Fold a piece of A4 paper or card in half. Write a story or poem and draw a picture about your story inside the card. Draw an elephant small enough to fit inside your folded card on another piece of card and cut it out. Cut a strip of paper as big as your finger and fold it like a concertina. Glue one end of the folded strip inside the middle of card and the other end to your character, when you open the card your elephant will pop out. Write a message inside the card.

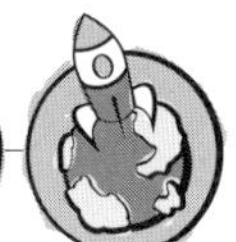

Passport Check

Why we like it

Through play you can learn about diversity, culture and the environment. Passport Check takes you to countries within the five continents of the earth.

What you might need

Card and paper to make passports
Pens
Paints
Old sheets dyed yellow
White material and polystyrene pieces
Material to dress up as a Polar bear
Brown paper bag
Heavy book and newspaper.

How many can do it

2–10.

Where you can do it

Outdoors or indoors.
Preparation time is needed.

How you can do it

1. Make a passport. Fold an A4 sheet of paper or card in half. Decorate the front of the passport with either your name or a picture as identification. Draw a picture of yourself or stick a photograph and sign your name.

2. Choose a country to visit and imagine what you might see there. Take Australia for example. Koalas live in the eucalyptus forests. The nocturnal marsupial spends most of its life in trees and has special paws to help it climb. Make a print of a Koala.

3. Cover a table with newspaper. Tape a square of felt, rubber or heavy cotton onto the table (squares from the back of a rubber lined carpet work well). Draw a Koala climbing eucalyptus trees with a wax crayon onto the fabric or rubber. Make the wax markings quite heavy and the lines quite thick.

4. Mix up water-based paints with a little water to thin it slightly. Using a roller or a wide soft brush paint the whole of the felt or rubber.

5. Press a piece of white paper onto the design and rub gently.

6. Slowly separate the paper and your print. Repaint the print and make more pictures. You can wipe the rubber stamp to apply a different coloured paint, but you will need to make more stamp templates if using cotton or felt.

7. Stamp your passport with your first visit to Australia, stick in your print or draw pictures of what you have discovered.

8. Move to your next destination.

9. Why not visit Africa next? When visiting the continent of Africa you could make some tree pulp art. Cut a large brown paper bag into a square or shape of your choice. Soak the paper in a bowl of water. Carefully wring it out and lay on a sheet of newspaper. Cover with newspaper or towels and place a heavy object such as a heavy book and leave to dry. When dry you will have a tapa cloth or bark cloth, a common fabric made with tree pulp. Using marker pens and paints draw patterns found in nature. Use watercolour paints to colour in your patterns.

10. Whilst in Africa visit the Sahara Desert. The Sahara Desert is the largest desert in the world. Make an imaginative play area of the desert. Using a sheet of yellow material, cover pillows to make dunes. Put a bowl with water at the edge of the desert surrounded by pot plants. Make a sun to hang from the ceiling over the desert. Write about the adventures that you had in the Sahara in your passport.

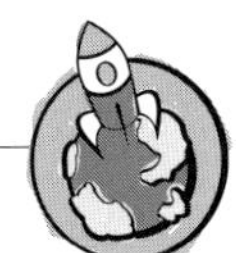

11. What about a colder country next? Wrap up warm to go to the North Pole in search of Polar Bears. Put on your coats and scarves. Cover the floor in polystyrene pieces and white sheets. Play the bear hunt: one player hides dressed up as a bear, the other players have to go through snow storms, go fishing, jump over the breaking sea ice, to find the bear. As the bear wakes the players must run away via the sea ice, fishing and snow storms until they reach the safety of their base where they can warm up in a scientist's cabin. Recover with ice lollies. Stamp your passport and record your adventures.

Useful Tip

Allow space for the imaginative play areas. If possible set up all the areas in one session so that you will have a sense of travelling from one country to another.

12. Continue your adventures in different countries.

Snapshot

During the summer holidays the Crows Nest playscheme held a travel session. The outside area was set up with different activities and experiences from different countries. The sandpit was turned into the Great American desert with cardboard cut-outs of cacti and rubber snakes. This desert is the hottest place on earth but it rains twice a year, the children visiting the desert were also rained on! The paddling pool was filled with polystyrene pieces and a glacier. Volunteers stood by with metal boards whipping up an eerie wind sound and a polar bear chased the travellers out of the Arctic and into east Africa. A mixture of imaginative exploration, arts and crafts, food tasting and native games resulted in very full passports.

What next?

Have a looking corner with interesting objects, pictures, and books from different countries. Introduce different foods at snack time.

Gravity Art

Why we like it

Everyone can take part. It is a sensory activity investigating movement. The finished product can be a fabulous piece of modern art! There are many opportunities to test different methods and painting techniques. A great activity to do in a group as it requires teamwork and co-operation.

What you might need

An empty washing up bottle or similar container

String

Poster paint

A large sheet of plain paper or card, no larger than the length of the broom handle

A broom handle

Old clothes to wear for painting

An open area.

How many can do it

You need a minimum of three participants.

Where you can do it

If is a fine day try this activity outside, remember to weight down your paper. The wind might add some extra paint effects!

How you can do it

1. Cut off the base of a clean and empty washing-up liquid bottle or similar container. It needs to have a lid and a nozzle.

2. Pierce or snip four holes near the cut edge, thread four pieces of string approximately 60 cm long and knot securely. The string will be used to suspend the bottle.

3. Mix up some poster paint with water to make it runny, so it will drizzle continuously. Pour the paint into the plastic bottle. Make sure the lid is on tight!

4. Arrange a space to do your painting—away from walls and furniture and not in a walkway. Lay your sheet of paper or card on the floor and put some weights on the corners such as pebbles. Protect surrounding floor with newspaper.

5. To suspend the bottle, tie the ends of the strings to the centre of your broom handle. Ask two people to hold each end. Make sure the bottle is hanging over the middle of the paper. Hold the bottle at an angle of 45° and remove the lid. Gently let the bottle fall and stand back.

6. You can investigate other painting effects by using different containers and more nozzles. Perhaps pierce lots of holes in the bottom of a container, cover the holes with tape until you are ready to paint.

7. You can do this activity on a smaller scale in pairs. Use a small plastic drinks bottle, pierce a small hole in the bottom of the bottle and cover with tape. Tie string to the bottle and suspend from a ruler. Fill the bottle with runny paint and hold above a piece of paper on a table. The other participant releases the bottle at an angle after removing the tape.

8. Make a colourful piece of art by repeating the above method with different coloured paints. Either wait for the first layer to dry or watch what happens when the wet paints mix.

What next?

Make picture frames for your gravity art.

Exhibit your pendulum paintings at your play setting.

Look at other activities to investigate gravity.

Useful Tips

Wear painting clothes

Make sure you have a clear space

Use washable paints

Arrange an area to dry the paintings

Safety Check

Adult supervision and assistance may be required for the cutting of plastic bottles and piercing hole.

Shadow Makers

Why we like it

Shadow Makers is a great activity that allows you to look and discover light and shadows. The pinhole camera allows independent inquiry while the shadow games require co-ordination and are lots fun to play.

What you might need

For the pinhole camera

a small cardboard box

thick brown paper or black sugar paper, card

a sheet of tracing paper

a drawing pin

masking tape

a blanket, towel or dark coloured material

black powder or poster paint

black felt pen.

For the Shadow play

A sunny day

Chalk and a paved or hardplay area.

How many can do it

1–7.

Where you can do it

Make the pinhole camera indoors. Play shadow games outside.

How you can do it

Pinhole camera

1. Cut both ends off the box using scissors. Paint the inside of the box with the black paint and decorate the outside.

2. Measure and cut a piece of brown paper slightly larger than the open side of the box. Tape the paper to one of the open sides once the paint is dry.

3. Cut a piece of tracing paper and tape it to the remaining open side.

4. Carefully pierce a hole in the middle of the brown paper. Keep the hole as small as possible.

5. Cover your head and the camera with a towel or blanket with the front of the camera peaking out. Hold the camera about 15 cm away from your face and point it to a window. You should see the upside down image of the window appear on the tracing paper.

6. To make your pinhole camera look more realistic try another version. Draw round a cardboard tube on one side of a rectangular box and cut out this circle. Cut a small viewing hole in the other end of the box. Cover one end of the tube with tracing paper and secure with an elastic band. Cover the other end with card, tape down and prick a small pinhole in the card. Insert the tube in the box with the end covered in tracing paper inside the box. Keep some of the tube outside the box to resemble the lens on a camera. Secure the tube with brown tape. Decorate the camera with buttons and features. Light only enters the camera through the pinhole, your head covers the viewing hole.

Useful Tips

Keep the pinhole as small as possible, a small hole will produce a sharp image. Experiment with larger holes to see how the image becomes blurred.

Spotlight—Rays of Light

Rays of light are straight and when these rays are blocked by an object, a shadow appears. The image in your pinhole camera appears upside down. This is because light from the top of the window passes in a straight line through the pinhole to the bottom of the tracing paper. Light at the bottom of the window travels to the top of the camera.

7. Making Shadows

Why do things have shadows? Play these games on a sunny day outside and find out:

Play catch with your shadows—is it better to run towards or away from the sun?

Make a monster shadow with your friends

Can you jump on your shadow?

Can you shake hands with your friend's shadow without touching each other? Can you make your shadow touch the top of a tree?

8. Shadow detectives

Become private detectives as you follow the mysterious movements of the 'Shadow'. The shadow has been accused of slowly travelling up and down the sides of the buildings and creeping across playgrounds and gardens. To collect substantial evidence you will need to plan an all-day stakeout as a supplement to other investigations. For this project you will need the sun, a shadow to trace—such as that of a tree, flagpole, or building—and a paved surface on which to draw with chalk. Start the investigation first thing in the morning. At first, shadows will be stretched out and long. Trace whatever shadow is cast on the pavement. Allegedly, shadows get shorter because the sun gets higher in the sky. Private detectives will have to check this out every hour by tracing the shadow and checking the sun's position. As you keep tabs on the sun's route, you might notice the shadows shrinking to almost nothing by midday and the reversing their position to grow again.

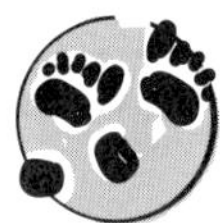

What next?

Draw pictures of the images you see through your pinhole camera.

Look at photographs and find out about how other cameras work.

What other methods can you find to make shadows? You could shine two torches, from different angles, on to an object and observe its shadow. What happens when you move the torches closer to the object and further away from the object?

Make a shadow puppet theatre using the torches and the shadow making techniques you have discovered. Cut out your own figures from dark card and attach to thin sticks. Make a screen using a white sheet hung over a doorway. Dim the lights and present your shadow puppet play to the audience.

Did you know...rays of light are straight. When these rays are blocked by an object such as a person or a tree, a shadow appears.